GENESIS 1-25
FROM START2FINISH

MICHAEL WHITWORTH

ISBN-10: 1941972705
ISBN-13: 978-1941972700

Published by Start2Finish Books
PO Box 660675 #54705
Dallas, TX 75266-0675
www.start2finish.org

Printed in the United States of America

Cover Design: Josh Feit, Evangela.com

CONTENTS

1

IN THE BEGINNING

GENESIS 1-2

Objective: To discover what the days of
creation teach us about the nature of God

INTRODUCTION

The Bible's account of creation is among its most majestic passages, stepping the reader through the origin of the cosmos, and
leaving us in inspired awe at all that God has done. The text does
not answer all our questions about the beginning of all things, but
that's okay—it wasn't meant to. It does, however, succeed at its main
purpose, which is to glorify God.

EXAMINATION

Read Genesis 1:1-2. Like any great book or movie, the first
sentence of the Bible is one of its most famous: "In the beginning,
God created the heavens and the earth." But though it is familiar to
us, the word-order in Hebrew is awkward, structured in a way that

highlights God as One without beginning or origin and unbound by time or space. Such ideas were unprecedented in ancient religions.

Just as we turn to science to explain how stuff works, ancient peoples used mythology to provide their answers. If you had asked an Egyptian or Canaanite, "Where does rain come from?" the response would have been a dramatic and elaborate tale about the rain god, not a physical science lecture. Every society has had its own cosmology—a creation story explaining the earth's origins—that served as the incubator for that society's world-view. In short, people tend to speak and act out of their answer to the question, "Where did I come from?" or "How was the world created?"

According to the Egyptians, there were no gods "in the beginning"—just primordial waters or a cosmic bowl of soup. Their god, Amun Ra, emerged from these waters and created the lesser gods through the secretion of some rather gross bodily fluids. In Babylon, the famous story *Enuma Elish* told of how the goddess Tiamat fought the youthful upstart god Marduk but was defeated. Marduk used her corpse to fashion the heavens and the earth. Humans were later created to provide slave labor for the gods. Other ancient creation stories illustrate this same low view of deity and humanity.

The most popular cosmology today, evolution, claims all things were created by chance. Human beings evolved over hundreds of thousands of years from tiny atoms swimming around in primordial waters, and the impersonal forces of luck, fate, and karma govern the world—not God. Evolution, the new paganism, is a product of man's desire to eliminate accountability to anything divine. If life is an accident of cosmic proportions, then we can all resort to a dog-eat-dog mentality—survival of the fittest—without any consequences. But Gen. 1:1 rescues us from these lies. The universe is not a result of chaos or warfare, but of God's orderly and peaceful design. In God, "all things hold together" (Col. 1:17).

Read Genesis 1:3-2:3. In ancient times, changing a name implied ownership and rule (cf. Gen. 17:5; 2 Kgs. 23:24). So God's sovereignty over all the earth is underscored by his bestowing names like "day," "night," etc. However, conspicuously missing are the Hebrew words for "sun" and "moon"—the generic phrases "greater light" and "lesser light" are used instead. Many people in ancient times worshiped the sun, moon, and stars, but by withholding their names, they are robbed of any claim to divinity.

From the creation of light, the narrative quickly moves through each successive day. Days 1 and 4 deal with light and the heavenly bodies. Days 2 and 5 detail the creation of the sky, sea, and their creatures. Days 3 and 6 discusses the formation of dry land and its creatures.

At the end of Gen. 1, man and woman are created. The prominence of this event starkly contrasts with ancient creation stories that portrayed man's creation as an afterthought. In Genesis, the creation of man is not an afterthought; it is the climax of the creation account. Notice:

- God calls the attention of his heavenly court to what he is about to do.
- While he had created everything by divine fiat up to that point, God formed man with his own hands. "Let there be..." gave way to "Let us make..."
- God deemed his creation "good" six times, but only after the creation of man did he call it "very good" (v. 31).
- God gave to Adam alone dominion over the earth and its inhabitants.
- Unlike the animals, Adam is the only creature to bear God's image.

This last concept is a heavy one to consider, and its implications are equally profound. In ancient times, rulers were thought to be the "image of the gods" (i.e. the gods' representatives on earth). However, this designation was never extended to the average Joe, so when Moses applied it to all humanity, the Genesis cosmology became all the more radical compared to its contemporaries. Because everyone was created in God's image, every individual is born with intrinsic value. It also means that everyone represents God's presence on earth. Such an awesome, even frightening, concept makes the biblical call to godly living all the more crucial: if we fail to reflect God's nature on earth, no other created thing is left to answer that call.

Only after his creation was "very good" did God rest from his work (2:2), though "rested" is a poor translation. The nuance of the Hebrew verb translated "rest" is one of ceasing and stopping, not relaxing and rejuvenating (cf. Josh. 5:12; Ezek. 16:41). Here, the seventh day is blessed and hallowed, but it would not become a mandatory day of "ceasing" until Sinai (Exod. 20:8-11).

Read Genesis 2:4-25. The theme of Gen. 2 may seem like a mere repetition of Gen. 1. But the creation account given here focuses on how God created a one-of-a-kind garden-home for Adam.

In a culture where the material of something designates its value (diamond jewelry, solid-wood furniture, leather interior), our being made from dirt should give us pause. But being made from dirt also expresses our glory because we are never told what material was used to fashion fauna, fish, and fowl. When it came to his crowning achievement, God decided to roll up his sleeves and actually get his hands dirty; he took what was insignificant and made life. And Scripture considers our being made from dirt as a sign of our dependence on God (Psa. 103:14), not just our relative insignificance.

Kings of antiquity often built magnificent gardens and temples adjacent to their palaces as monuments to their unsurpassed wealth. Eden is likewise depicted as God's garden-temple, filled with rich spices and precious stones (vv. 11-12), an earthly monument to his unsurpassed majesty.

A river flowed from Eden that later separated into four. The Tigris and Euphrates were important rivers in the Fertile Crescent, but the exact identity of the Pishon and Gihon are unknown. The Pishon has been speculated to be the Indus or the Ganges, while the Gihon is thought to have been the Persian Gulf or Red Sea. In a symbolic sense, these rivers represented God's life-giving presence flowing forth to all the earth.

Two of Eden's trees are singled out. The first made perpetual life possible for all who ate its fruit, and God never restricted access to it until after the Fall. However, the second tree was rendered off-limits from the beginning. What exactly was imparted by eating its fruit is still debated, but that is a discussion for the next chapter. What must be noted here is that God gave man the autonomous freedom to make his own decisions, and he did so presumably to discover what was in Adam's heart.

After Adam was created and placed in Eden, he was given the task of working and keeping the garden. Work is often thought to be a consequence of the Fall, but notice that in the perfect world that God created, man was created to work as a means of glorifying the Lord. We may suppress or neglect it, but the need to serve our Creator has been fundamental to our existence since the beginning (Eph. 2:10).

God had given Adam life, and a home, and a job, but he wasn't through yet. God noticed Adam's loneliness, and it is only at this point that God called something "not good" in his creation. He brought to Adam the animals he had created, and Adam gave names to each, but he did not find a suitable companion to aid him in fulfilling God's purposes. So God blessed his life with Eve, a woman formed from his ribs. Reflecting on the significance of being created from the rib, Matthew Henry eloquently observed that the woman was: "Not made out of his head to rule over him, nor out of his feet to be trampled upon by him, but out of his side to be equal with him, under his arm to be protected, and near his heart to be beloved."

Adam's response to the creation of Eve, "This at last is bone of my bones and flesh of my flesh" (2:23), highlights their equality and his feelings of incompleteness without her. Eve was, as is every godly wife, a true Godsend. And in that relationship of "one flesh" so unique to marriage, a man and woman can experience a hint of Eden's by-gone splendor.

APPLICATION

The Nature of God. The creation myths of ancient civilizations—especially how they depicted their respective gods—betrayed the values of those cultures. Likewise, Israel's cosmology in Gen. 1-2 also says a lot about their God. For example, in these chapters we learn that Yahweh is a God who loves order and structure. He created all things in perfect sequence and ordained that all things reproduce after their kind. He is also sovereign over all things, and all things came into being through his spoken word. God does not have to manipulate or strive—only to speak—in order for his will to be accomplished. The apostle Paul later claimed that God's eternal power and divine nature are witnessed in the natural world (Rom. 1:20; cf. Psa. 19:1). The natural world, when viewed through the lens of Scripture, has much to teach us about God's nature. The Bible's creation account is of profound importance in our quest to better understand the nature of God.

The Value of Creation. It was not unusual for ancient civilizations to claim that their regent bore the image of the gods. What was unusual (even unheard of) was for anyone to claim that all people were made in God's image, but this is exactly Genesis' claim. More than that, all of us have in ourselves the breath of life put there by the Lord. It is illogical to say that all human life is sacred, that all are created equal, and that all are endowed with certain inalienable rights unless we also affirm the other truths of Gen. 1-2, namely that there is a Creator who values every life as masterpieces borne of his heart. Most everyone has heard the title of Charles Darwin's famous work *Origin of the Species*, but few know the complete, original title: *On the Origin of Species by Means of Natural Selection, or the Preservation of Favoured Races in the Struggle for Life.* From its inception, the theory of evolution has been consistent with a world-view that favors one group of people over another. Just as ancient cosmologies fostered moral decay, modern evolution has corrupted the value of human life, most notably the lives of the "least of these." Any appeal to human rights must be based on the confession that every human being has been created in God's image.

Remember the Sabbath. Christians no longer observe the Sabbath as Israel once did. Even Sunday, sometimes considered the Christian Sabbath, is not shackled by the same rules. "These are a shadow of the things to come, but the substance belongs to Christ" (Col. 2:17). This means the Sabbath principle still holds great importance for God's people. Reality is indeed found in Jesus, one who regularly escaped the routine so that he might partake of the holy (Mark 1:35). Following his example, every Christian should find ways to pause the weekly grind and commune with the Father. God prohibited Israel from working on the Sabbath to remind them that he was really in charge. If the world survived when God rested, things wouldn't fall apart when Israel did the same. Christians also need a reminder that all things are held together by God. This is our Father's world, rather than our own.

CONCLUSION

Before we rush to the remainder of Genesis, it would do us good to pause and reflect. It is here, in the first words of Scripture, that God is exalted to the highest of places: sovereign Creator, supreme Ruler, and compassionate Father. Moses' comment that the man and his wife were naked, but they were not ashamed (2:25), draws the curtain on a universe as God intended it, and underscores the sad reality that things have shifted violently off course since then. The evil that plagues the human condition is conspicuously absent "in the beginning." There was a time when everything was in total subjection to God's will. But in light of the Fall, we can only look forward to the day when God will unite all things in heaven and earth under the sovereignty of Christ (Eph. 1:10).

QUESTIONS FOR REFLECTION

1. What is Moses' primary objective in the first two chapters of Genesis?

2. Why are the creation stories of a society/civilization important? What do they answer or provide?

3. What is the predominant creation story in modern America? Is it at odds with the Bible's creation story? How so?

4. In the biblical world, what did bestowing a name represent?

5. What does it mean that God "rested" on Day #7?

6. What was the only thing not "good" about God's original creation? How did he rectify the situation?

QUESTIONS FOR DISCUSSION

1. Read Psa. 19:1 and Rom. 1:20. What else can we learn about God's nature solely from the created world?

2. What does it mean that humans are made in God's image?

3. Who is the "us" of Gen. 1:26?

4. Though we are no longer obligated to do so, why is it good to rest regularly as God did on the seventh day?

5. God made Eve out of Adam's side—what does this say about God's will for the marriage relationship?

2

THE RISE OF SIN

GENESIS 3-5

Objective: To explore how sin entered
the world and its effects on us all

INTRODUCTION

As a book of origins, Genesis tells us all about the existence of
evil. It is thus natural to wonder, "Have things always been this way?
If not, when did evil enter the world? Is God responsible?" The re-
sounding chorus of "good" and "very good" in Gen. 1 teaches us that
the world as God created it was perfect, so something dreadful must
have occurred after the fact.

With their rebellion, Adam and Eve levied unspeakable hardship upon this small planet. Their oldest son murdered his brother in
cold blood, and his descendants grew even more depraved. Genesis'
first genealogy highlights the scourge of sin and death on the human
race with the refrain "and he died."

But in the midst of so much evil, the light of grace kept shining.

Though God granted free will to his people, he did not allow wickedness to hold hostage his plan for reconciliation. God continued to work out his will in the world.

EXAMINATION

Read Genesis 3. Various legends in ancient times attempted to explain man's loss of immortality. In one story, a god name Ea deceived the man into refusing food that would have given eternal life. In another, *The Epic of Gilgamesh*, the hero obtains a magical plant that bestows immortality, but it is stolen away and swallowed by a snake.

In both these stories, immortality was lost by man due to robbery or trickery, but not by any fault on man's part. In contrast, that is a picture wholly inconsistent with the one presented in the Bible. According to Genesis, death is a product of nothing less than our own rebellion against God.

In Gen. 3, the serpent's strategy in deceiving Eve was:

1. To misrepresent God's word and heart. The serpent focused on God's *prohibition* without mention of God's *provision*.

2. To smuggle "in the assumption that God's word is subject to our judgment," according to Derek Kidner. But this would mean God is no longer Lord.

3. To create doubt in God's desire for intimacy with us and the belief that God is not concerned about our welfare.

What is arguably most disturbing about this story is that Adam was with his wife the entire time. Adam at least heard the conversation and could have prevented his wife from yielding to temptation, but he just stood there.

As he regularly did, God arrived to walk with the first couple in the evening breeze. He asked where they were hiding, which is ironic because he had to have known the answer already. God was giving Adam and Eve the opportunity to own up to their sin—which they eventually did, but not before engaging in a pass-the-buck form of protest. Neither took any real responsibility.

The biblical concept of "curse" has nothing to do with hexes or magical incantations. Rather, as John Walton puts it, "to curse is to remove from God's protection and favor." In a scene reminiscent of a criminal trial, God cursed the most important relationships to the serpent, the woman, and the man:

1. God cursed the serpent's relationship with itself. It is condemned to crawl and be associated with dust, a position of abject humiliation.

2. God cursed the woman's relationship with her children and husband. Painful childbirth and the rule of her husband shall be her lot.

3. God cursed the man's relationship with his wife (she desires to dominate him) and his work (the ground is cursed).

As an act of grace, God provided garments of animal skins for Adam and Eve to cover their now-shameful nudity; he did for them what they could not do for themselves. But he was also forced to drive them from the garden, and he stationed at Eden's entrance cherubim wielding a frightening sword of fire to prevent their return to God's presence. Such intimate access to God would not be restored until the death of Christ (Matt. 27:51).

Read Genesis 4. We are not told why Cain and Abel offered sacrifices to God, or even how they learned proper worship protocol. Nor is it easily apparent why Cain's sacrifice was rejected and Abel's accepted. But upon further investigation, the answer lies in the quality of the offerings. Abel's offering was from the firstborn of his herds (v. 4), while Cain didn't exactly bring his best.

The significance of 4:7 cannot be overstated. Sin is vividly personified as a monster of the darkness, a predator (1 Pet. 5:8) waiting to ambush Cain and devour him. Sin desires Cain, i.e. it desires to subdue and devour him. But it is also very much within Cain to defeat sin as a man would defeat a wild animal.

Though he was warned by God to keep his anger in check, Cain brutally murdered his brother in retaliation. The narrator describes the scene with unexpected brevity, but two details we learn elsewhere add significantly to the picture.

First, the Law of Moses later stipulated that a crime committed out in the fields was proof that the offense was premeditated (Deut. 22:25–27). What Cain did was not a momentary lapse in judgment; it was calculated murder. Second, in 1 John 3:12, the apostle rejected the conventional Greek verb meaning "to murder" and opted for another verb that means "to slaughter or butcher." Rather than a simple knock on the head, we are to imagine an enraged Cain hacking his brother to pieces with merciless brutality.

After the murder, God mercifully invited Cain to confess his actions, but Cain coldly shrugged off any responsibility for his brother. Only then did God call Cain to realize that "the voice of your brother's blood is crying to me from the ground" (v. 10). In those words, an important pillar of biblical theology is established: innocent bloodshed must be atoned lest it corrupt the ground and disperse the divine presence.

Cain whined that his punishment was unreasonable. He was frightened at the prospect of leaving his family behind and facing would-be assassins (most likely Abel's descendants, if there were any) seeking to avenge his brother's murder. Cain was concerned more with his punishment than his crime. Yet in an act of grace similar to the garments given to Adam and Eve (3:21), God promised Cain protection symbolized by a "mark." We are not told exactly how God marked Cain, so we must conclude that it is immaterial to the story. The Lord subsequently banished Cain from his presence, and Cain journeyed east.

It is assumed that Cain married a sister or other close relative. He was blessed with a son, Enoch, and Cain named the city that he founded after him. In the subsequent genealogy, Cain's family is traced all the way to Lamech, the first bigamist, and his three sons. An unfortunate incident is recorded about Lamech, after which he bragged that he killed "a young man" who simply wounded him. By exhibiting such vindictive arrogance and excessive brutality (not to mention disrespect for monogamy in marriage), Lamech proved that Cain's descendants had become increasingly depraved.

Read Genesis 5. By listing the generations connecting Adam and Noah, this chapter bridges their stories. The author follows a particular template in recording the biography of each patriarch, and with only a few exceptions, the formula is the same:

- Father's age at first son's birth
- Years lived after birth of first son
- Notice of other children
- Sum total of years lived
- Notice of death.

We are also immediately impressed with the incredible length of human life in the pre-Flood world. Jared, Methuselah, and Noah all lived more than 950 years; only Mahalalel and Lamech failed to reach 900 years. But these lengthy lifespans are significantly muted by the refrain "and he died," a harsh, poignant phrase that reminds us of the judgment under which we all live because of sin.

Enoch and Noah are the only ones in this genealogy to receive special attention, and Enoch's biography is the most unique. He is the seventh (a significant biblical number) generation listed from Adam. It is twice mentioned that Enoch "walked with God" (5:22, 24), a phrase indicative of a life lived in harmony with God and his will. The normal refrain of "and he died" is conspicuously absent from the account of Enoch's life. Instead, the text says "he was not" and "God took him" (5:24), meaning Enoch was raptured to heaven without dying, as was Elijah (2 Kgs. 2:11-12).

APPLICATION

An Act of Grace. The gift of garments to the first couple (3:21) was certainly an act of grace on God's part. But could it be that banning their access to the tree of life (3:22) was also an act of grace? With sin having now invaded the world, perhaps it behooved a merciful God to make immortality an impossible achievement. One can imagine the horror of someone like Herod, Hitler, or Hussein living forever; their reign of terror would know no end. Human suffering would be even more enormous than it already is. The deaths of evil tyrants remind us that no matter the severity of the suffering, there comes a time when it will end. Barring the way to the tree of life seems to us as punishment, but it could also be affirmation of a God who graciously gives us what we need: an anticipated finality to the misery of our sin and its consequences in the world.

Confession Is Good. The first two sins in Scripture bear many similarities, not the least of which being God holding the offenders accountable for their actions. There is within us all not just the desire to sin, but also the tendency not to own our sins. Some do this by practicing a robust self-righteousness, but this makes us no friend of God. Yet others avoid owning their sins by making excuses. By listening to our excuses, one would think that our sins are always someone else's fault. But maintaining a biblical view of sin requires us to confess our guilt. Reconciliation with the Father is impossible as long as we deny ownership of our transgressions (1 John 1:8-9). A confessed sin, no matter how terrible, is never beyond the forgiveness and redemption that God so graciously offers us.

Walking With God. That Enoch was the only one in Gen. 5 to escape the plague of death should not escape our notice. It certainly did not elude the author of Hebrews (11:5–6), who eloquently noted that Enoch's faith made him pleasing to God. In our present culture, people will flock to athletic clubs, avoid food preservatives no one can pronounce, and obsess over their caloric intake in an effort to cheat death as long as possible. But "while bodily training is of some value," faith and godliness are the only true ways by which we can escape this world and inherit the one to come (1 Tim. 4:8; 1 John 5:4). Our faith is to be in Jesus, who violently destroyed death at the cross (2 Tim. 1:10); as was modeled by Enoch, godliness is to be expressed by an intimate walk with the Lord.

CONCLUSION

The final significant note of Gen. 5 is Lamech naming his son, Noah. The patriarch looked back to the agony that had afflicted man's work since the Fall and longed for God to bring relief from the curse. It might be that Noah, whose name means "rest" or "comfort," was thought to be the one who would bring fulfillment to the promise of Gen. 3:15. And relief would indeed come in Noah's lifetime via a global Flood and a cleansed earth. But relief from the curse of death would not come through Noah; that would have to wait until the dawn of Christ's resurrection. By virtue of the resurrection, we have the unfailing hope that we will one day have access to the tree of life and live forever in God's glorious presence.

QUESTIONS FOR REFLECTION

1. What was the serpent's strategy in deceiving Eve?

2. What is the biblical concept of a "curse"?

3. How did God show grace to Adam, Eve, and Cain in their sin?

4. What did God specifically warn Cain about concerning sin?

5. What is the conspicuous recurring phrase in Gen. 5?

QUESTIONS FOR DISCUSSION

1. How did God curse the most important relationships to the serpent, Eve, and Adam respectively? How do we see the effects of this curse even today?

2. How is the curse of death also a gift of grace?

3. Why was Cain's sacrifice rejected and Abel's accepted?

4. How did sin spread/compound through Cain's family tree?

5. Who is the only person in Gen. 5 to escape death? Why? What hope does this hold out to God's people?

3

NOAH & THE FLOOD

GENESIS 6-9

Objective: To appreciate the severity
and grace found in Noah's story

INTRODUCTION

The story of Noah's ark is among the most well known in Scripture. Regardless of whether one accepts as fact all biblical claims concerning the deluge, it's pointless to deny that there was an unprecedented flood many, many years ago—a litany of flood stories have been preserved from civilizations in Europe, Asia, and even North America.

However, it is quite puzzling to me that the story of Noah's ark has become such a favorite for young children. Its artwork adorns nurseries and Sunday school classrooms, and its figurines make for great fun at bath time. But by making Noah's ark so popular with kids, have we also conferred on this narrative too much cuteness or innocence? Think about it. In the words of James McKeown, what we have in the Noah narrative is "a horror story in which human beings—men women, and children—and innocent animals are swept away by merciless floodwaters."

Yet even in his justified wrath, God could not bring himself to destroy all of creation, so he preserved Noah's family. In the text, we discover that the preservation of those eight souls aboard the ark was 100% God's work of grace.

EXAMINATION

Read Genesis 6. The beginning of this chapter is a prologue of sorts explaining why God decided to destroy the world. The corruption and violence on earth had become greater than he could tolerate, and he was forced to execute judgment. Noah and his family would be delivered from the impending destruction, but only because Noah found grace in God's eyes (6:8) and was obedient (6:22).

Two very strange phrases appear in the prologue. First, who are "the sons of God" and "the daughters of man" (v. 2)? Second, who are "the Nephilim" (v. 4)? Suffice it to say that the answers to these two questions have been intensely debated through the centuries with three alternatives emerging.

- "Sons of God" = angels (cf. Job 1:6; 2:1; 38:7). Under this view, the sins of the angels was a transgression of boundaries, and humans were culpable by their willingness to intermarry with angels.

- "Sons of God" = lineage of Cain. This would make "daughters of men" the lineage of Seth. The sin here is intermarriage between the wicked and the righteous.

- "Sons of God" = ancient rulers who practiced polygamy and promiscuity with the women of their kingdoms, i.e. the daughters of men (not unlike the medieval practice of prima nocta).

As for the Nephilim, these seem to have been ancient warrior-heroes, offspring of the angel-human union.

Despite all the mystery surrounding this passage, one thing that is abundantly clear is the world's corruption had reached such a critical mass that God was forced to act. God "regretted" creating mankind, a complicated word that can mean "repent" or "change one's mind" in certain contexts. But here, it conveys shock and sorrow over a corrupted creation God had once declared to be "very good."

But in an act of sheer grace, he singled out Noah, a man through whom the entire human race would be preserved. God instructed Noah to build an ark, a box-shaped barge without rudder or sails. It was constructed out of "gopher wood," possibly an ancient term for cypress, a common rot-resistant material used in shipbuilding in the ancient Near East. The ark was to measure 450 feet long, 75 feet wide, 45 feet high, with a total deck area of about 95,700 square feet. A cubit's-width opening or gap was left at the top of the ark, and a door was added. Conspicuously missing is any mention of a rudder or sails: the fate of all aboard would be solely in God's hands.

Noah was also instructed to take a pair of every unclean animal and seven pairs of every clean animal, enough food for the voyage, and place all these in the ark. The comment, "Noah ... did all that God commanded him" (v. 22), highlights the fact that Noah was an individual determined to do his Creator's will.

Read Genesis 7-8. To our knowledge, the ancient world had never seen rain until this time (cf. 2:5; Heb. 11:7)—at least rain in this volume. The impending disaster was a result of God's righteous condemnation of the world. At the same time, the survival of Noah's family was not an accident, but an intentional act of divine providence.

Four times (7:18, 19, 20, 24), the Hebrew *gabar* is used, meaning "prevailed." It is used elsewhere in the Old Testament as a military term. Here, the floodwaters acted as the army of the Lord, dispensing his justice and punishment on a corrupted planet. All life was extinguished. In the Flood, there is a reversal of the Creation story.

- Whereas in Gen. 1 "God saw everything that he had made, and behold, it was very good" (1:31), now "God saw the earth, and behold, it was corrupt" (6:12).
- The Lord brought the animals to Noah (6:19–20; 7:2–3) as he had for Adam (2:19).
- The expanse separating "waters from the waters" (1:6) was removed, and "all the fountains of the great deep burst forth, and the windows of the heavens were opened" (7:11).
- God had given the breath of life to his creation (2:7); it was now taken away (7:22).

In his wrath, God reversed the work of his hands because of its wickedness. But in his mercy, God restored his creation because of his great love. The first act of Creation had been God's Spirit moving on the water's surface (1:2); the first act of restoration after the Flood was God's Spirit moving on the water's surface (8:1).

When the ark finally came to rest on dry ground, it had been six months since raindrops first began to fall. Noah's family waited an additional 75 days before the peaks of surrounding mountains were visible (8:4–5). Forty days later, Noah sent out a raven, a dove, a second dove, and then a third dove to discern whether the waters had receded; this was actually a common method used by ancient seamen in order to find land. When the second dove returned with a fresh olive branch in its beak, Noah knew that his time on the ark was coming to an end. The third dove failed to return at all. So it was that, almost a year after Noah's family had entered the ark, God beckoned them to exit onto dry ground.

In gratitude for his family's survival, Noah offered sacrifices. God swore to himself that he would never allow the preceding disaster to repeat itself, though the human heart was in the same evil state as it had been before the Flood (6:5; 8:21).

Read Genesis 9. For the first eight chapters of Genesis, mankind had been vegetarians, but this exclusive practice came to an end when God gave Noah and his family permission to eat meat, though the blood had to be properly drained first (vv. 3-4). To insure that the sanctity of life was not devalued in the process, capital punishment was ordained for those who shed innocent blood, and not even animals were exempt.

God blessed Noah and his family, commanding them to spread out and repopulate the earth (vv. 1, 7). He also made a covenant with Noah, revealing his previous oath to never again destroy the world with a flood (8:21).

As a reminder of the covenant, God placed a rainbow in the sky. The Hebrew word translated "rainbow" can also refer to the warrior's weapon. It was not uncommon in ancient times to depict deity as holding a warrior's bow (e.g. Psa. 7:12; Lam. 2:4; Hab. 3:9). In Genesis, God placed a warrior's bow in the heavens with an arrow symbolically pointing towards himself, and he entered into a contract with Noah on pain of death. As Tremper Longman III notes, "Of course, God can't die, and that is precisely the point. He can't break the covenant either."

Later in life, Noah became "a man of the soil" (v. 20) who planted a vineyard. He then made wine and became intoxicated. While Noah lay nude in his inebriation, Ham dishonored his father by leering at him (cf. Hab 2:15) and then telling his brothers. The Hebrew verb used here means to look at in a searching way—certainly not innocuously or unintentionally. In contrast to Ham's deplorable actions, Shem and Japheth honored their father by covering him.

Patriarchal blessings and curses are a regular feature in Genesis. A father's words had a lot to do with the destiny of his son and his posterity. They are not to be necessarily considered pronouncements from God, but they nonetheless held prophetic sway over future events, and were considered irrevocable (27:37). That's why Noah cursing his son is so noteworthy.

Why would Moses include such a bizarre story in the Genesis narrative? It explains the moral depravity of Ham's lineage. In Lev. 18:3, God condemned the sexual promiscuity of Egypt and Canaan, both of whom descended from Ham (Gen. 10:6). Following that mandate in Leviticus is a list of sexual taboos of which both Egypt and Canaan were guilty, expressed more than a dozen times in terms of uncovering a relative's nakedness. So this disturbing story explains how Ham's descendants tragically lost their moral compass.

APPLICATION

The Nature of Sin. At its root, sin is a transgression of God's boundaries, but it is more than that. When we sin, we break God's heart. The wickedness of Noah's day made God deeply troubled (Gen. 6:6), and our sin affects God in the same way. Sin is not a sickness that needs to be medicated, a personality disorder that needs to be treated, or a blunder we can flippantly dismiss with "Everyone makes mistakes." Sin is an offense and abomination against a holy God. More than a cute children's story, may the story of Noah's Flood impress upon us the high cost of sin and the great severity of God's righteous judgment.

Power of Repentance. Could the Flood have been avoided had the wicked responded to Noah's preaching with repentance? In Genesis, the pattern has been for God to announce judgment and punishment before dispensing it, as if giving his people a chance to repent and avert disaster. We never learn whether Adam, Eve, or Cain repented of sin. On the other hand, when God commissioned Jonah to preach a message of judgment and doom, nothing was ever said about God relenting on his decision if Nineveh repented. But that is exactly what they did, and God spared them (Jonah 3:6-10; cf. Jer. 18:7-10). For us, even though God has already announced judgment for the wicked, "if we confess our sins, he is faithful and just to forgive us our sins and to cleanse us from all unrighteousness" (1 John 1:9).

The Earth's Destiny. Proponents of global warming claim the melting polar ice caps will flood the globe and wreak havoc on the planet. However, God has stated that such will never again happen, and we know God's Word never fails (Isa. 55:11), nor can he lie (Heb. 6:18). Scripture calls us to steward the planet's resources if for no other reason than it is God's possession (Psa. 24:1), but Christians are also assured that the business of the world will go on until God's people hear a trumpet and a loud voice in the sky. Everything will once again be destroyed as it was in Noah's day (2 Pet. 3:10), but it won't be of concern for the people of God since we will, at that point, already be with the Lord forever (1 Thess. 4:17).

CONCLUSION

The Flood story is indeed horrible and a testament to the righteous wrath of a holy God. Everything was destroyed. But the Flood story is equally a testament to God's grace. He preserved Noah and his family out of mercy. He promised never again to destroy the planet with a flood out of mercy. Next time you see a rainbow in the sky, "Note then the kindness and the severity of God: severity toward those who have fallen, but God's kindness to you, provided you continue in his kindness" (Rom. 11:22).

QUESTIONS FOR REFLECTION

1. Though many focus on the obscure reference to "sons of God," etc., in the Flood's prologue, what is the real main point of those first eight verses?

2. What is the significance that the Ark clearly had no rudder or sails?

3. How does the author present the Flood as an undoing of creation?

4. What did the rainbow represent?

5. What significance did patriarchal blessings in Genesis hold?

QUESTIONS FOR DISCUSSION

1. How has the Flood story taken on an inappropriate innocence?

2. Why is it important to think and speak of sin as God vs. the world does?

3. Why did the author preserve the embarrassing story of Noah's drunkenness?

4. Why can Christians have hope in the face of various doomsday scenarios (e.g. Red Scare, Y2K, global warming)?

5. How and why are secular Flood stories vs. the biblical Flood story so different despite their similarities?

BABEL & THE NATIONS

GENESIS 10-11

Objective: To learn how God used human
arrogance to further his scheme of redemption

INTRODUCTION

Our corrupted, fallen world loves drawing distinct lines of division based on race or ethnicity, education level or socio-economic status, language or dialect. Regrettably, the Lord's church has not been immune to this. But our differences shouldn't necessitate division, for we "are all one in Christ Jesus" (Gal. 3:28).

Indeed, Gen. 10-11 proves that God faithfully works out his redemptive plan through multiple generations and across countless centuries, and that he cares intimately for those of every skin color, language, and nationality. In Gen. 10, seventy nations are listed, but all of them have both a common father and a common Creator. In Gen. 11, those nations were scattered by God across the face of the planet due to linguistic differences brought on by their pride and arrogance. At that point, it seemed as if the world was destined again for total destruction, just as it was in the days of Noah. But as it turned out, God had other ideas.

EXAMINATION

Read Genesis 10. Seventy different nations are listed here, making it easy to understand why this chapter is so often called the "Table of Nations." Because we are dealing with a very ancient list, identifying and locating all of these nations is impossible; for some of them, scholars can only make semi-educated guesses. But generally speaking, Japheth's family settled in Europe and Asia Minor, Ham's family in Palestine and Africa, and Shem's in what is now considered to have been the Fertile Crescent.

The list begins with the descendants of Japheth who settled the farthest away from Israel and had contact with them the least. Some of Japheth's children spread out between the Aegean and Caspian Seas. Others settled along the northern coast of the Mediterranean, perhaps as far as the Iberian Peninsula, and also populated the Mediterranean's numerous islands.

The lineage of Ham populated much of Africa and Palestine. "Cush" is most often identified with Ethiopia (Jer. 13:23), and "Put" with Libya. Of specific interest to Israel would have been the descendants of Ham's youngest son, Canaan. Sidon was the oldest Phoenician city, located on the Mediterranean coast north of Tyre. Heth was the father of the Hittites, who must be distinguished from the empire of the same name that once existed in modern-day Turkey. The Hittites of the OT dwelt in Canaan's hill country, and it's probable that these are the people Moses had in mind. The Jebusites, Amorites, Girgashites, and Hivites are all known to have lived in Canaan (Deut. 7:1). The other nations mentioned were located in Palestine or were Phoenician colonies scattered throughout the Mediterranean world.

Those from Shem settled in an area stretching from the Arabian Peninsula to the Black and Caspian Seas, but mostly along the Tigris and Euphrates; generally speaking, they were the ancestors of those who later spread to the remainder of Asia. The name Eber became the origin for the term *Hebrew*. His son's name, Peleg, means "to divide," which explains the editorial note that "in his days the earth was divided" (v. 25). It's likely that it was during Peleg's life that the Tower of Babel was built, and God subsequently introduced linguistic divisions on the earth.

One particular person of interest in this chapter is Nimrod (vv. 8-9). Reference is made to an early Hebrew legend about this man's exploits that has since been lost to us, but it appears Nimrod was an ancient version of Chuck Norris. Nimrod's name can mean "we shall rebel," and Jewish tradition considered Nimrod to be the inventor of idolatry and the leader of those who built the Tower of Babel. He is certainly credited with establishing some of the greatest cities of the ancient world, including Babylon and Nineveh (vv. 10-12).

Read Genesis 11:1-9. The previous chapter illustrated where the various nations ended up; this story tells how they got there. Attention shifts to "a plain in the land of Shinar" (called "Sumer" in ancient texts). Noah's descendants left Ararat and journeyed east, which in Genesis is often indicative of a separation from God (cf. 3:24; 4:16; 13:11).

Rather than a spiraling tower such as the one depicted in Gustave Doré's 1865 engraving *The Confusion of Tongues*, the Tower of Babel probably resembled the ziggurats discovered by archaeologists in modern-day Iraq. They were built to resemble large mountains and were centers of religious activity for ancient Mesopotamian cultures. Unlike the pyramids of Egypt, ziggurats in Mesopotamia were completely filled with dirt and had a façade of kiln-fired brick. Each one had a stairway or ramp that led to the summit where a little room had been constructed with a bed and table. This was where the gods would lodge as they made the journey from heaven to earth.

The pivotal moment in the story is when God arrived on the scene (11:5). Perhaps tongue-in-cheek, the narrator writes that God had to come down to see what was being done, despite the fact that the tower was supposed to stretch up to the sky. The construction project was clearly a human initiative, and a puny, pathetic one at that. The Lord issued a summons to the angels to join him in spreading confusion. He injected disunity into the builders' midst by confusing their language. No longer would one person find it easy to understand another.

As a consequence, the building project fell off for a time, and the citizens of Babel went their separate ways, clustering into clans based on language. The narrator ends with another tongue-in-cheek reference to the etymology of "Babel." Whereas the citizens of Babylon claimed that the name of their great city meant "the gate of the gods," Moses says it derived from the Hebrew *balal* meaning "he confused."

One question that arises from the text is this: what exactly was Babel's sin? From childhood, I was always told that it was their disobedience of God's command to fill the earth (1:28; 9:1). Their fear was that they might "be dispersed over the face of the whole earth" (11:4). But it has been argued that when God said to multiply and fill the earth, he meant it as a blessing, not a command; the Hebrew can certainly be translated this way.

Was Babel's pretension and hubris their sin? In the text, God muses that in light of the people's great numbers and unity, "this is only the beginning of what they will do. And nothing that they propose to do will now be impossible for them" (11:6). So God subsequently divided them into separate nations and languages to limit the grave impact of consolidated wickedness.

There is some truth to both suggestions. If the punishment was dispersion, it seems disingenuous to argue that their sin had nothing to do with disobeying the command to "fill the earth." Given the great wickedness that God observed before the Flood, it seems justified to assume that Babel's threat was too much evil in one place.

But there is one more aspect to Babel's sin than these options provide. Scripture says that these people settled at the site of Babylon to "make a name" for themselves, something only the Lord is allowed to do (Neh. 9:10; Isa. 63:12; Jer. 32:20). The citizens of Babel sought to bring glory to themselves at God's expense, and that is wrong (Isa. 42:8). Babel's choice to congregate in evil, rather than fill the earth in righteousness, was symptomatic of their refusal to make God their king and give him praise. When we seek our own agendas instead of God's, we share in Babel's folly.

Read Genesis 11:10-32. With the close of this chapter, the patriarch Abraham enters the biblical spotlight. His father Terah was an idolater and pagan (Josh. 24:2, 15), which should come as no surprise since his home was Ur of the Chaldeans, a major center of moon-worship in ancient times. In addition, the names Terah, Milcah, and Sarai are all related to worship of the moon god Sin.

In Abraham's day, Ur would have been a once-grand cultural center now declining due to economic hardship and overpopulation. Its remains reveal that it had several important structures, including lavish royal tombs and a massive ziggurat. Its close proximity to the Persian Gulf likely means the city's wealth derived somewhat from maritime trade.

Whenever the flow of a genealogy is interrupted, we should pay attention, and the detail of Sarai's (Sarah's) barrenness is an important one to future narratives. Barrenness was a grave condition in ancient times, one synonymous with abject hopelessness. But in what would become a recurring theme of Scripture, God was prepared to deliver hope to his people in the midst of their despair.

APPLICATION

Brotherhood of Man. We sometimes treat strangers in ways we would never treat family or close friends—with rudeness, arrogance, or cruelty. But as Gen. 10 demonstrates, the entire world is one big family with a common father in the first man, and a common Creator in the God of heaven. The late evangelist Marshall Keeble was famous for commenting on the brotherhood of man by quipping, "If I miss him in Christ, I'll hit him in Adam." Indeed, Jesus' Golden Rule is illogical apart from the claim of Genesis that every human being shares a common ancestry in Adam and Noah. This alone should inspire all Christians to reevaluate their treatment of others. Our call is to exercise acceptance, patience, forgiveness, submission, and love—not only because that is what God did for us in Christ, but also because that's just how you should treat family.

Lost in Translation. When we hear the language or accent of another nationality, it is natural for us to grow frustrated and for ethnocentric arrogance to rear its ugly head. But instead of getting all in a bind, perhaps it would do us good to pause and consider why linguistic differences exist in the first place (sin), and how they point to our need for a Savior who, at the end of time, will hear "every tongue confess" him to be Master (Phil. 2:11). That same Savior, so I've been told, loves all the little children of the world—red and yellow, black and white. We should endeavor to do no less, regardless of our differences, for we are all precious in his sight.

The Blessing of Division. God hates division, but he is not above dividing us in order to teach us to rely more fully on him. There is no denying that the Bible is in favor of unity, something for which Jesus specifically prayed on the eve of his crucifixion (John 17:21). But note that Jesus qualified that request with, "May they also be one in us." Unity at any cost is not God-honoring unity. To be sure, the citizens of Babel were united, but it was a unity opposed to (rather than working for) the will of God. Attempts to maintain the unity of Jesus' body at the expense of truth or righteousness will always be frustrated by a holy God intent on purifying his Son's bride.

CONCLUSION

These two chapters concerning the post-Flood world carry a stark reminder that God cares about all nations. It would appear to anyone that the earth was populated by means of happenstance wandering, but it was in fact the product of God's design.

Centuries later, exiled Israel would discover comfort in passages like Gen. 10-11. God had most assuredly not abandoned his people. Israel had only to wait for him to further unfold his redemptive plan to unite all nations and peoples under the reign of his Holy One, a plan that would culminate in "every tongue [acknowledging] that Jesus Christ is Lord" (Phil 2:11 NIV). This plan commenced with the call for Abram to leave his father's house.

QUESTIONS FOR REFLECTION

1. In what general areas did the descendants of Shem, Ham, and Japheth settle respectively?

2. Why would the Israelites be particularly interested in Ham's descendants?

3. 3.   What/who is the origin of the word *Hebrew*?

4. What ancient building did the Tower of Babel likely resemble?

5. The names Terah, Milcah, and Sarai were all related to the worship of what god?

QUESTIONS FOR DISCUSSION

1. How does Gen. 10 include a call to treat strangers, even those of different nationalities, as family?

2. Why is it frustrating when trying to communicate with someone who doesn't speak our language? What should such occasions remind us of?

3. In your opinion, what exactly was Babel's sin?

4. Though in most instances God hates division, why is division sometimes a blessing and unity a curse?

5

FATHER OF THE FEARFUL

GENESIS 12, 20

Objective: To examine Abraham's many struggles
with faith and how he overcame them

INTRODUCTION

The patriarch Abraham casts a formidable shadow across the
pages of Scripture. Israel's religious heritage, material inheritance,
and ethnic identity were all associated with Abraham. At times, it
was for Abraham's sake that God chose not to destroy Israel, for he
was remembered as God's friend (2 Chr. 20:7). In the New Testament, inspired writers consistently point to Abraham as the ultimate
example of one who is faith-full, so it is easy to see how Abraham's
name became synonymous with faith itself.

But Abraham's faith, long acclaimed as the ultimate model to
emulate, had as many hiccups as highlights. His relationship with
God was peppered with doubt and failure. We often stand in awe of
the great heroes of faith, men like Noah, Moses, or David, and say,
"My faith could never be that great." But when we actually read the

stories of these heroes in the text, we are caught off guard by their human frailty, and that should encourage those of us who periodically struggle to trust God.

EXAMINATION

Read Genesis 12:1-3. After the death of his father, Abraham received God's call to pick up and move to a new land, the land of Canaan. That Abraham did so was a dramatic move on his part. In the ancient world, to leave your father's house was to forfeit one's inheritance and claims to family property. More than that, Abraham was being asked to forsake the gods of his father's household (Josh. 24:2) and to worship God Yahweh alone. He was asked to surrender home, family, and faith—things that are so fundamental to a person's identity— that was a tall order. But some very special promises came coupled with the command to "Go." It is important that we delineate these promises, for they are collectively the lens through which we must view all of Abraham's life. These four promises were of:

PROPERTY. The promise of land, of property, drives the narrative of Abraham's life beginning in Gen. 12. He arrives in the land, only for it to be plagued with famine. He returns to Canaan in Gen. 13, only for it to appear insufficient for both his and Lot's herds. In Gen. 14, foreign militaries threaten Abraham's peaceful existence in the land. Throughout, God kept promising that all of Canaan would be given to the patriarch and his descendants (12:7; 13:15, 17; 15:18-21), culminating in the oath of 17:8. But Abraham himself would never legally own a single divot of sod in Canaan except for his own grave (23:17-18; 25:9). And his descendants wouldn't possess Canaan until after suffering four centuries "in a land that is not theirs" (15:13).

POSTERITY. God later added that Abraham's descendants would become a nation as innumerable as sand and stars (13:16; 15:5; 22:17). Implicit in this was also the promise of a son (15:4), though

Abraham and Sarah had no biological children at the time (11:30). But if the promise of property drives the narrative of Gen. 12-15, the promise of a child drives it in Gen. 16-21. Abraham's frustration over being childless is a regular source of conflict. He arguably thought that Lot would be his heir until the latter moved away in Gen. 13. In Gen. 15, Abraham seems indignant that the replacement heir is a servant in his household. In Gen. 16, he thinks the tension to have been resolved with the birth of Ishmael. Even after Isaac was born, this promise continued to drive the narrative as the patriarch was called to offer this unique, special son as a sacrifice back to God. This is the promise with which the patriarch arguably struggled the most.

PROSPERITY. This is the one promise that never caused a problem for the patriarch. He never had to wait and never experienced a lack of faith in this matter. Abraham would go on to receive from foreign kings gifts of silver, gold, and large flocks of animals. He would enjoy possession of certain "status symbols" such as camels. He was even able to afford a 318-man private security force.

PROTECTION. God promised, "Him who dishonors you I will curse" (12:3; cf. 15:1). Though the ESV distinguishes between the two, most English translations of 12:3 disguise the difference between the first and second use of "curse"—e.g. "whoever curses you I will curse" (NIV). The words are different in Hebrew. The first meant to disdain or despise and refers to verbal harassment; the latter "curse" signifies a formal legal conviction of sin similar to God's curses on the serpent, Eve, Adam, and Cain.

Read Genesis 12:4-20. Abraham embarked on a month-long journey of over 500 miles. Once in Canaan, he first stopped in Shechem (generally regarded as the geographical center of the Promised Land), and camped near a distinct oak tree in that region. God's reaffirmation of his promises led Abraham to commemorate the occasion by building an altar.

After staying in Shechem for a time, Abraham journeyed 23 miles south to Bethel, a place that housed a shrine to the Canaanite god El. The patriarch spurned the thought of showing customary honor to this false god and instead worshiped the true God at this place. With Abraham's later movement into the Negeb (the arid land southwest of the Dead Sea), he completed a tour of the whole Promised Land from north to south.

Several scholars have noted the frequency of famine in Palestine if seasonal rainfall does not fall in necessary volume, and average annual rainfall in the Negeb is only 4–12 inches anyway. Contrast Palestine and its fickle seasonal rainfall, with Egypt where the land is fertilized each year by the much-more-reliable Nile floodwaters. Consequently, Egypt was noted in Scripture for its relatively stable food supply (Deut. 11:10).

In spite of her 65 years of age, Abraham considered Sarah's striking appearance a liability while living in a foreign land. When they had left Haran, they had agreed to deceive when necessary in order to protect Abraham's life (20:13). His plan seems to have been to pose as the brother in order to intercept any marriage plans.

When the Egyptians noticed Sarah's striking beauty, she "was taken" to Pharaoh. The text is unclear whether sexual intercourse actually took place. It seems she was added to Pharaoh's harem, one way or another, and Pharaoh awarded Abraham with a substantial bride price of livestock and servants. The gift of female donkeys and camels were particularly valuable.

No sooner had Sarah been taken than God cursed Pharaoh and his house with "great plagues." The king was understandably upset with Abraham, who had put him at risk by deceiving him. It is a foreign, pagan monarch who is concerned with this breach of morality, not Abraham! His silence during the interrogation effectively betrays his guilt. In his justified anger, Pharaoh could have just as well had Abraham executed for his deceit. As it was, however, Pharaoh expelled him from Egypt in a manner similar to God's exile of Adam and Eve from Eden (3:23). In a desperate attempt to save his own life in a foreign land, Abraham almost lost it.

Read Genesis 20. Twenty-five years later, Abraham found himself in a similar situation. For much of that time, he had been living near Hebron (13:18), but he now moved on, journeying as far as the Sinai Peninsula before doubling back to Gerar. At Gerar, the ruler Abimelech noticed Sarah and took her as his wife just as Pharaoh had done, but this time the text is explicit that intercourse did not take place (v. 4).

In a dream, God condemned Abimelech for taking Sarah, though Abimelech had done so with a clear conscience (20:6). God made clear that, if Sarah were not returned to her husband, severe punishment would be imminent. As it was, the Lord had already struck Abimelech's harem with barrenness, and had afflicted Abimelech himself with some sort of sexual dysfunction (vv. 17-18).

Like Pharaoh, Abimelech was justifiably outraged with Abraham's blatant deception and thus interrogated him. This time, Abraham explained the reasons for his actions, confessing that Sarah was his half-sister and that fear for his survival had motivated him to lie about his marriage. To make reparations, Abimelech gave the patriarch livestock, servants, and a thousand silver shekels. He also allowed Abraham to live and travel throughout the land without harassment, something Pharaoh had not conceded (12:20). Note, however, the very sarcastic way Abimelech says to Sarah, "I have given your brother..." not "I have given your husband..." It seems the king resented what Abraham had done.

In both stories, it's not clear what Abraham planned to do should someone ever claim Sarah as a wife. If he lied about his marriage, then Sarah being taken as someone else's wife was inevitable.

He placed his wife at risk for adultery, and in ancient times, adultery was known as "the great sin" (cf. v. 9) and often legislated against. What, then, did Abraham hope to accomplish, other than the preservation of his own life? We just don't know.

What is clear, however, is that Abraham refused to completely trust in God's promises. The Lord had affirmed that he would provide Abraham with protection when necessary (15:3), and would curse anyone who dared mistreat the patriarch (12:3). What need did Abraham have to lie in order to save himself? Whether his plan was a well-thought-out scheme—or a poorly devised, last-minute ploy— Abraham refused to trust, and that decision blew up in his face.

APPLICATION

Take Up Your Cross. When Abraham embarked from Haran, he became the first of many to enter the wild frontier of faith. To succeed, Abraham had to leave his old life behind. He had no doubt grown comfortable in Ur and Haran, but all of that comfort had not given him the one thing he desired most: a child and a future. Before they know it, Christians can become too comfortable to do what faith requires: too cozy in a relationship we have no right to be in, too cozy with a habit that is not consistent with godliness, too cozy with a career that is leading us away from the heart of God. Relationships are important, habits are hard to break, and paychecks put food on the table, but they can also hijack an incredible opportunity to trust in God with our whole heart and see what great things he might do to rescue us from our silent despondency (Prov. 3:5-6). We are thus presented with the dilemma—the great paradox—of faith: the only way to abandon hopelessness is to abandon all else but God.

An Example to Unbelievers. When we act faithlessly, we negatively impact those around us. We cannot be faithful carriers of God's blessing to the nations also being faithless to God's will. It is speculated that the Pharaoh of Gen. 12 was Wahkare Achthoes III (c. 2120–2070), a pharaoh who wrote several proverbs, some of which warned against the treachery of people from Asia—such as Abraham! Had Pharaoh's experiences with the patriarch colored his perception? The apostle Peter urged his readers "as sojourners and exiles to … keep your conduct among the Gentiles honorable, so that when they speak against you as evildoers, they may see your good deeds and glorify God on the day of visitation" (1 Pet. 2:11–12). Abraham did not walk with integrity during his sojourn in Egypt or Gerar. By God's help, may we be better examples to the unbelievers around us.

Amazing Grace & Patience. More overwhelming than Abraham's deceit is God's devotion. As Paul put it, "if we are faithless, he remains faithful—for he cannot deny himself" (2 Tim. 2:13). Abraham's moral failures did not earn for him instant damnation. Indeed, we are bothered by the very absence of censure of the patriarch. Isn't lying a violation of one of the commandments (Exod 20:16)? To be sure, there is nothing to be emulated in these stories, but the greatest take away might be that God is more patient with us than we sometimes imagine (Psa. 103:14; cf. 1 John 3:20). We must never confuse this as being God's tolerance of sin, but rather an acknowledgment from the Lord that nothing worthwhile happens overnight. Spiritual growth takes time! Sanctification can't be microwaved. We must content ourselves with the reality "that he who began a good work in you will bring it to completion at the day of Jesus Christ" (Phil. 1:6).

CONCLUSION

These stories, along with their parallel in Isaac's life (26:6–11), are problematic because the narrator never censures the patriarch. Did God approve of the deception? Such is hardly likely, for God hates falsehood (Prov. 6:17). We are not in a position to judge Abraham, but we should take these episodes as examples of Walter Scott's admonition, "Oh what a tangled web we weave when first we practice to deceive." The patriarch simultaneously put in jeopardy his wife and God's promises, and it was only the Lord's intervention that gave both stories a happy ending.

We have no right to expect God to do the same for us, but we certainly have every confidence in his willingness to forgive us graciously. This is where our story merges with Abraham's, the wonder of a God who at times stands between sin and consequences, and mitigates or abolishes our penalty when we deserve his full wrath. There is no word in any language to adequately describe such grace. "Amazing" will have to do.

QUESTIONS FOR REFLECTION

1. What four promises did God make to Abraham when he called him to leave his father's house?

2. Of the four promises, which one was fulfilled completely with no "waiting" and no lack of faith?

3. Abraham's three stops in Canaan were Shechem, Bethel, and the Negeb. What was the combined significance of these three places?

4. What was Abraham's reasoning for posing as Sarah's brother vs. her husband?

5. What did Abraham receive from both Pharaoh and Abimelech in exchange for Sarah being taken?

QUESTIONS FOR DISCUSSION

1. How have you struggled to trust God's promises in your life?

2. Explain what this statement means to you: "The only way to abandon hopelessness is to abandon all else but God."

3. How have you seen the faithlessness of God's people drive unbelievers away?

4. In trying to save his life in a foreign land, Abraham almost lost it. Have you been guilty of something similar? How so?

5. How has God been faithful to you in spite of your faithlessness? In what ways has he given second chances to you that you knew were undeserved?

6

ABRAHAM & LOT

GENESIS 13-14

Objective: To learn the value of being a peacemaker
and patiently waiting for God to keep his promises

INTRODUCTION

From fraternal conflict between Cain and Abel, to congregational strife in first-century Corinth, the Bible is no stranger to our human proclivity towards squabbles and spats. One such story is about Abraham, Lot, and their decision to separate so as to prevent a minor frustration from escalating into a major family feud.

But despite what you may have learned in Sunday School, the narrative of Gen. 13 is not primarily about how and why to be a peacemaker. Rather, this section of Genesis demonstrates how God began eliminating all obstacles in order for Abraham and his descendants to inherit the Promised Land. Terrible as conflict often is, the Lord is not above using it to further his purposes in the world.

EXAMINATION

Read Genesis 13. After Abraham and his entourage had been escorted to the Egyptian border by Pharaoh's guard, they traveled another 200 miles back to the Negeb. Abraham's material wealth is mentioned (v. 2) to set the stage for what happens next. Specifically noted is his possession of silver and gold, which means the patriarch held liquid assets that endowed him with financial stability in harsh economic times.

For the first time, specific details are given about Lot. He was also rich in livestock (v. 5), but silver and gold are not mentioned as they were in his uncle's case. The land surrounding their encampment simply could not support both of their herds. Mention of the Canaanites and Perizzites (v. 7) meant that others already occupied the land, so that is why they were so hard-pressed for adequate pasture.

Abraham is to be commended for addressing the quarrel in its early stages while it was still between the herdsmen. In addition, he took the high road by offering his nephew first choice when they decided to part ways; there is never an excuse to be selfish with God's blessings. As so today, ancient custom would have dictated that Lot defer to his uncle as the senior party. But Abraham was selfless because he trusted God to care for him, regardless of the quality of land in which he resided. He valued his relationships over his real estate.

Facing the east, Abraham encouraged his nephew to look north ("the left hand") and south ("the right hand") and choose a land to call his own in order to resolve the present conflict. Notice Abraham's words carefully; it seems that he intended for he and Lot to partition the land of Canaan between them. But Lot looked east (straight ahead, not to "the left hand" or to "the right hand"), and his gaze fell on the Jordan Valley. He surely knew that it was the choice land since it was not dependent upon seasonal rainfall for nourishment. This valley was so ideal that the narrator went out of his way to compare it to Eden. But whatever illusions of paradise we might thus conjure up are immediately dashed with a reminder that the infamous Sodom and her sister cities were located on this plain (v. 10).

Nonetheless, Lot chose the fertile valley as his new home, parted ways with his uncle, and settled near Sodom. The move meant that Lot was now leaving Canaan, the land of blessing and promise. His move in the direction of the east again invites the observant student of Genesis to consider Lot as moving away from God (cf. 3:24; 4:16; 11:2). Abraham's nephew was clearly choosing common sense over faith.

After Lot made his ill-fated decision, God rewarded Abraham's peaceable spirit by expanding upon his prior promises. Whereas the promise of land had previously been a general "the land that I will show you" (12:1), it was now specified. Likewise, the promise of posterity had previously been a general "I will make of you a great nation" (12:2). Now it became a promise to make his descendants impossible to number.

The command to traverse the land (13:17) is reminiscent of ancient customs pertaining to the legal acquisition of property. Upon his coronation, a new king would often tour his kingdom as a way of establishing his sovereignty. A related custom may be reflected later in the OT: God assured Joshua, "Every place that the sole of your foot will tread upon I have given to you, just as I promised to Moses" (Josh. 1:3; cf. Deut. 11:24), and in Ruth 4:7, Boaz sealed a real estate transaction with the exchange of sandals, again reflecting the idea of acquisition by traversing the land.

Read Genesis 14. We are accustomed to imagining the patriarch as a peaceful pastoralist—a tent-dwelling hybrid of Santa Claus and Mister Rogers. But this chapter violently presents us with Abraham the Hebrew warrior. However, this story illustrates yet again how God made good on his promise to bless, provide for, and protect the patriarch. In the narrative, we also glimpse growth in Abraham's character; he values kinship and disdains illicit rewards. He is maturing as a man of faith before our very eyes.

The chapter is a tale of four kings going to war against five kings. Twelve years prior, the five cities of the Plain had been subjugated by an alliance led by the ruler of Elam, Chedorlaomer. After being vassals for a dozen years, the five kings rebelled. In response, Chedorlaomer marshaled his allied forces and embarked on a military campaign. Pillaging as they went, Chedorlaomer's forces finally met their opponents, the armies of Sodom and her sister cities, in the Valley of Siddim.

This valley was full of bitumen ("tar" NIV) pits; when Chedorlaomer routed the army of the five kings, they fled into the hills, and some of the soldiers fell into these tar pits by accident and perished. In the aftermath, Chedorlaomer and his allies made off with prisoners and loot from the five cities. Since he was now "dwelling in Sodom," rather than simply living in the general vicinity (13:12), Lot was among the POWs.

A messenger brought to Abraham news of the battle and the fate of his nephew, and the patriarch saddled a posse. In a scene reminiscent of Gideon (Judg. 7:8-25), the posse pursued the allied armies "as far as Dan," attacked at night and completely routed Chedorlaomer's army, recovering prisoners and loot alike. Returning home from battle, Abraham was greeted by both the king of Sodom and Melchizedek, the "king of Salem," in a place called "the King's Valley" (cf. 2 Sam. 18:18), an area two and a half miles south of Jerusalem. The king of Sodom brought nothing with him to Abraham; on the other hand, Melchizedek produced bread and wine to duly honor Abraham as a royal guest and conquering hero.

That Melchizedek "was priest of God Most High" emphasizes that he and Abraham had a mutual faith in the God of heaven. There is little doubt that, in his blessing, Melchizedek attributed Abraham victory to the sovereignty of God. Abraham's subsequent tithe was thus an expression of gratitude to God for victory, and to Melchizedek for his blessing.

In very stark contrast to Melchizedek's grand generosity, the king of Sodom demanded Abraham return the people and keep the plunder for himself. Melchizedek's first words in the narrative are "Blessed be Abraham," while the king of Sodom's are "Give me!" But the patriarch had no desire to keep anything that did not belong to him—not even "a thread or a sandal strap." Abraham had once before allowed himself to be enriched at another's expense (12:16), and it had not ended well. Here, Abraham would claim no right to Sodom's plunder except the provisions his men had already consumed.

APPLICATION

Blessed Are the Peacemakers. When we pursue peace in the midst of conflict, our efforts help fulfill God's plan for the world. Whether or not he realized it, by opting for a peaceful solution in Gen. 13, Abraham made it easier for God's will to become reality. This same principle is echoed in Paul's letter to Rome. After rehearsing God's grand scheme of redemption to bring the Gentiles into the church (Rom. 9–11), Paul implores his readers to live transformed lives (12:2) characterized by humility (12:3–8), love (12:9–13), and peace in the face of conflict (12:14–21). Paul infers that seeking revenge interferes with (but does not thwart) God's will. Vengeance is God's; let him extract it. We may think that, by opting for peace, we are doing "nothing." But as Abraham Lincoln famously said, "The best way to destroy an enemy is to make him a friend." When we prove ourselves peacemakers, we do more than vengeance ever could. Though it seems a paradox, laying down the sword and extending the olive branch of peace could be the most courageous thing we ever do.

Fearful vs. Faithful. Settling for the short end of a stick in any disagreement isn't easy. It had to have annoyed Abraham just a little when his graciousness was abused by Lot's greed. Christians are supposed to be magnanimous, but it doesn't always work out that way. The church at Corinth suffered from an epidemic of lawsuits, a problem of which Paul was quite critical (1 Cor. 6:1-8). Opting to suffer instead of sue, however, depends on how much faith we have in God vs. fear of the unknown. When Abram said to Lot, "Let there be no strife between you and me" (13:8), the word used for "strife" was *meribah*, the name Moses gave to the place where Israel quarreled in the wilderness (Exod. 17:1-7). The linguistic link between these two stories reminds us that we have two options when things don't go our way: fear or faith. Fear causes us to complain out of our disappointment. Faith causes us to confess our dependence. Fear is the conviction that, if I was taken advantage of, then God didn't come through for me. Faith is the conviction that, if I was taken advantage of, then God must have something greater prepared for me in the future. Fear behooves us to reach out and take control. Faith motivates us to "let go and let God," confident that he is as benevolent as he is sovereign.

Patience with God's Plan. It is significant that the patriarch is called "Abram the Hebrew" (a term often identifying a person as a foreigner) in the narrative (14:13), but never again in the Bible. Used here, it called attention to the fact that Abraham was a stranger in a strange land. But since he expelled the victorious Chedorlaomer from Canaan, Abraham had a legitimate claim to Canaan. God had already promised it to him (13:17)—why not seize it all now with his obviously superior fighting force? But that's the thing about biblical faith—it sometimes requires us to surrender the bird in our hand for God's two in the bush. We sometimes struggle with overreaching in regards to God's promised blessings. Our world of instant gratification has conditioned us so. Biblical faith demands that we be patient as God's plan unfolds his way, instead of jumping the gun and prematurely grabbing what God has promised—which is exactly what Abraham does in Gen. 16.

CONCLUSION

There is much to learn from Abraham's example in these two stories. He was magnanimous in seeking peace with Lot; after defeating Chedorlaomer, he did not greedily seize by force what was rightfully his (Canaan)—rather, he was willing to wait on the Lord's timing to receive the promised blessing.

The Lord's goodness to Abraham in this story also must not be overlooked. While it appeared that Abraham's family had fractured with Lot's departure, God was using conflict to work out his plan. Whenever we deal with conflict, we must conduct ourselves in a way that glorifies Christ, confident that God will use such negative events to accomplish his purposes in the world and glorify his great Name. More than a story on how to be a peacemaker, Gen. 13-14 reminds us that God honors peacemakers by making them a part of his grand scheme of redemption.

QUESTIONS FOR REFLECTION

1. Why is it mentioned that the Canaanites and Perizzites were in the land with Abraham and Lot (13:7)?

2. Facing the east, Abraham told Lot to look to the left and right to choose a new place to live. Why is this significant?

3. What land did Lot chose instead? Why?

4. Why did God command Abraham to walk the boundaries of Canaan (13:17)?

5. By soundly defeating the new conqueror of Canaan (Chedorlaomer), what was Abraham technically entitled to?

6. What was the difference between Melchizedek's and the king of Sodom's treatment of Abraham?

QUESTIONS FOR DISCUSSION

1. How do we help to further God's work in the world when we make peace?

2. Why is making peace often the most difficult, courageous thing we will ever do?

3. How is seeking revenge or payback an act of fear? How is forgiveness an act of faith?

4. Lot chose common sense over faith. How have you been guilty of the same?

5. In what ways have you been tempted to overreach with God's promises instead of being patient? How are you preparing yourself to "wait on the Lord" the next time this temptation arises?

7

THE BANK OF FAITH

GENESIS 15

Objective: To explore how and why Abraham was justified by faith

INTRODUCTION

This chapter is one of the most important in Abraham's story. The promises of property and posterity, soil and seed, merge here as never before. In fact, the theme of the Promised Land, which has dominated the previous chapters, will climax here and then recede into the background; meanwhile, the promise of offspring is reintroduced and subsequently assumes center stage.

But this chapter is important for another reason also. In v. 6, a statement is made concerning Abraham that sends shockwaves throughout the New Testament. In Romans and Galatians, Paul seizes upon the statement to illustrate how we are justified by faith, not works. As the father of the faithful, therefore, Abraham has much to teach us.

EXAMINATION

Read Genesis 15. Not long after vanquishing Chedorlaomer, God spoke to the patriarch in a vision, affirming Melchizedek's blessing. A militaristic theme runs through God's word to Abraham; besides the obvious "shield," "reward" refers to the loot a soldier would carry from the battlefield. In the previous story, Abraham had voluntarily forfeited his share of the victor's "reward" to Sodom's king, and considering Sodom's extravagant wealth, such plunder would have been quite valuable. Yet God affirmed that Abraham had walked away with something more precious than gold.

But as Abraham heard those words, the scab of an old wound apparently fell away to reveal raw frustration. What good was God's reward when the patriarch had no one to whom he could pass on the blessing? Twice in the opening verses, Abraham gives voice to this painful frustration. "What will you give me, for I continue childless, and the heir of my house is Eliezer of Damascus?" (v. 2). From a literary standpoint, that would have been enough to remind readers of Abraham's plight.

Yet the patriarch seemingly begs God to really, truly, actually consider his dilemma. "Behold, you have given me no offspring, and a member of my household will be my heir" (v. 3). One would have to forgive the patriarch for feeling vexed; God wanted Abraham to trust in his goodness, but in the world of Genesis, God's favor was manifest in multiple descendants (cf. 1:28; 9:1; 26:24; 35:11), and the Old Testament elsewhere considers childlessness to be God's curse (Lev. 20:20-21; Jer. 22:30). You and I have felt this tension of faith—it is the struggle to believe in God's favor in the face of his apparent failure (or worse, his displeasure).

It was not uncommon in ancient times for a childless man to adopt a son as his heir in exchange for the adoptee agreeing to discharge certain responsibilities expected of a son (e.g. care in old age, funeral preparations). Abraham likely had planned to adopt his nephew, Lot. But now Abraham apparently believed he would have to resort to making his chief slave the heir to his estate. And as common as it might have been for a man to adopt an heir in childless situations, to adopt one's own slave for this purpose was significantly less common.

In response to Abraham's complaint, God made a grand declaration to Abraham that clarified his earlier promise to make Abraham into a great nation (12:2). He assured the patriarch that, literally, a son would be granted to Abraham from his loins (v. 4). At that point, God countered Abraham's challenge to "Look" (v. 3) with his own: "Look toward heaven, and number the stars, if you are able to number them … So shall your offspring be" (v. 5; cf. 22:17).

The next verse (v. 6) is among the most important statements in the Old Testament, at least in view of its use in the New Testament. "And he believed the LORD, and he counted it to him as righteousness." To believe God, as it says Abraham did, means "to rely on someone, to give credence to a message or to consider it to be true, to trust in someone." More significantly, God credited righteousness to Abraham as a bank teller credits an account following a deposit. After some of his past (and future!) failures, Abraham had no hope of laying claim to moral righteousness on account of his actions. But God did for Abraham what the patriarch could not do for himself; he declared Abraham "righteous" by virtue of his faith.

On the heels of God's promise of a child came reaffirmation of the promise of land. Abraham's request for a sign (v. 8) should not be interpreted as a lack of faith—quite the contrary! That the promise might be firm in Abraham's mind, God commanded him to bring five animals.

At the heart of what happens next is an ancient ceremony whereby two parties entered into an agreement. The details vary in ancient literature, but the basic scene that emerges is of two people walking between the carcasses of slaughtered animals, striking an agreement, and wishing on themselves the same fate as these dead animals if their respective ends of the pact were not fulfilled.

Such ceremonies were apparently so prevalent that they affected the lingo; when it says that Yahweh "made a covenant" with Abraham (v. 18), it literally reads that he "cut a covenant" with the patriarch. From elsewhere in the ancient Near East comes similar phrases such as "to kill a donkey foal" and "cut the neck of a sheep" that mean the same thing.

And if all of this seems hopelessly antiquated, or an extreme way of sealing a deal, bear in mind that self-imprecatory oaths are not as foreign as they seem—witnesses in court are still required to take an oath to tell the truth, the whole truth, and nothing but the truth, "so help me God" (i.e. "If I lie, may God punish me"). I personally have heard more than a few people use the phrase, "If I'm lyin', I'm dyin'." Again, what God and Abraham did here is not that antiquated.

In what follows, the narrator intends for us to imagine a rather ominous scene, one pregnant with expectation of what God would do. It is a dramatic crossroads where fear and faith collide. As they are prone to do, "birds of prey" gathered on the slaughtered animals, and Abraham had to drive them away. This detail seems an odd one to mention unless we consider it an omen of Israel's enemies lurking like buzzards to devour them. The notion isn't far-fetched: Egypt's Pharaoh identified himself with the god Horus who was depicted as a falcon. And as we soon will learn, dark days lay ahead in Pharaoh's land for Abraham's offspring.

Elsewhere in the Old Testament, when we read the words "deep sleep," it often suggests "awe-inspiring divine activity." It was into a deep sleep that God placed Adam when he created Eve (2:21), and Abraham likewise slumbered as God acted mightily to allay the patriarch's fears.

Israel's future enslavement in Egypt must have caused Abraham great distress. Is there any consolation in one's seed becoming a great nation if they also become the neighborhood whipping boy? There is such consolation if God promises a mighty deliverance (v. 14).

But why was there a need for Israel to spend 400 years in Egypt? Why not cede Canaan to Abraham's descendants immediately? It was because, from God's perspective, "the iniquity of the Amorites is not yet complete" (v. 16). Another translation reads "the wickedness of the Amorites will not have reached its full measure until then."

To affirm all of this, the presence of God in the form of "a smoking fire pot and a flaming torch" moved between the halved animal carcasses. Consistent with the cultural practice, God presumably assumed upon himself the sentence of death should he not keep his promise to the patriarch. And no, God can't die. But God can't break his promises either (Heb. 6:18), and that is precisely the point. Israel's future possession of Canaan (its boundaries and present inhabitants listed in vv. 18-20, nullifying any ambiguity) was as sure a thing as God's eternality.

APPLICATION

Four-Century Delay. God gave notice that the Promised Land could not be inherited by Abraham's descendants until the sin of the Amorites was complete (v. 16). It is easy to assume that the God of the Old Testament was concerned exclusively with the Jews, but his sovereignty and concern knew (and knows) no political boundaries (cf. Psa. 47:7-8). Meanwhile, both in biblical and ancient secular literature, the Amorites' abhorrent depravity is well attested. This, then, is yet another testament to God's matchless mercy. Rather than execute immediate judgment, his delay betrayed his hope for Amorite repentance (2 Pet. 3:9). When some read Joshua's account of Canaan's conquest, they impose upon the text a caricature of a capricious, vindictive deity ordering the genocide of a peaceful, indigenous people. But what kind of God gives a nation four centuries to get their moral act together? One who is as loving as he is sovereign, and as gracious as he is holy.

Faith in God's Goodness. One of two central tenants to Abraham's story was the promise of children. God had promised to make Abraham's name great and make him into a great nation. But nearly a decade had passed since God had made these promises and Abraham had nothing to show for it. In addition, the one he thought would inherit his estate, Lot, was gone, and he was left with a servant as his heir. Abraham struggled to believe in God's favor in the face of his apparent failure or displeasure. At times, it is a struggle to believe that God is reliable, that he will keep his promises, when it appears that the evidence before us denies this truth. As human beings, we are accustomed to evaluating all of life via our five senses, but faith is at odds with our five senses (cf. 2 Cor. 5:7). At other times, we are tempted to believe that God has gone back on his promise because he is forcing us to endure his displeasure (at least as we perceive it). In all these moments, we must have Abraham's faith—we must believe, despite the "evidence," that God is good, that he is faithful, that he is always at work for our good and his glory, and that he is faithful to us even when we are faithless. In this way, faith is indeed the victory that overcomes the world (1 John 5:4).

Patient for Blessing. Whenever we are made to suffer, or whenever God seems lax in keeping his promises (or both), we often ask, "Why?" Why doesn't God rain down justice? Why doesn't God honor his word? Why doesn't he show us kindness? According to v. 16, it might be because God has not seen fit in his wisdom and mercy to remove his blessing from another. Abraham's offspring could not inherit Canaan just yet because God had not yet removed his blessing of land from the Amorites. Do you find yourself in a situation from which you have prayed for God's deliverance? Do you consider your present circumstances "suffering" and the other side to be "blessing"? It may be a zero-sum situation, one in which your gain is another's loss. God may not yet be willing to remove that blessing from another person. Perhaps his/her salvation hangs in the balance. Your willingness to patiently wait on the Lord could mean the salvation of a precious soul (2 Pet. 3:9). And isn't that the greatest blessing of all?

CONCLUSION

Centuries later, an anonymous historian in Israel would make this seemingly trivial comment. "Solomon ruled over all the kingdoms from the Euphrates to the land of the Philistines and to the border of Egypt" (1 Kgs. 4:21). It may be hard to believe, but until that time, Israel's borders had never been so broad or encompassed so much territory. Through many dangers, toils, and snares, God had kept his promise.

And God will keep another promise made to us, the children of Abraham living 4,000 years later. Through faith in Jesus, God has sworn to credit righteousness to us (Rom 4:24), though we are so undeserving. In God's ledger, we are all in the red. We are all deficient. But in response to our deposit of trust in him, he ascribes to us Christ's riches. He moves us into the "balanced" column, reconciled by his grace.

QUESTIONS FOR REFLECTION

1. What frustration did Abraham express in vv. 2-3?

2. What important promise did God reaffirm in v. 5?

3. What was Abraham's response (v. 6)?

4. By passing between the halves of dead animals, what was God promising to do regarding Abraham?

5. Why could Abraham's descendants not yet inherit the Promised Land?

QUESTIONS FOR DISCUSSION

1. Read Rom. 4. What does it mean that Abraham was justified by faith? What does this mean for us?

2. Christianity operates like a bank: we invest our faith in God, and in response, he credits righteousness (something we don't deserve) to our account. What worldly things do people often put their faith or trust in other than God?

3. God effectively gave the Amorites 400 years to get their moral act together—what does this tell us about God and his nature?

4. In what ways have you struggled to believe in God's favor in the face of his failure or displeasure?

5. In the past, how might God have made you be "patient for blessing"?

8

ABRAHAM & HAGAR

GENESIS 16-17

Objective: To explore the messy consequences of doubt
and God's grace in spite of our faithlessness

INTRODUCTION

In these chapters, we see Abraham caught up in the tension
between daring faith and doubt-riddled fear. One moment, he was
trusting that God could make his descendants as numerous as the
stars. The next moment, he was passively acquiescing to his wife's
attempts to circumvent God's miraculous and benevolent provision,
and that event caused a lot of problems, some of them still lingering
even into modern times.

Most anyone who has studied the Middle East eventually con-
cedes that it is a proverbial mess with no clear resolution, at least
none that will pacify all parties for very long. When Abraham fathered a son by Hagar, he created this very mess. But God remained
faithful to him, even when the patriarch was faithless. The Lord got
involved and promised to bring redemption to the situation.

EXAMINATION

Read Genesis 16. In the previous chapter, Abraham had been the one to express frustration at his childlessness; here, it is Sarah's agitation that drives the narrative. Barrenness was nothing short of devastating for women of antiquity. Like her husband, Sarah was caught between faith at either God's apparent failure or his devastating displeasure. Her grief was compounded by the knowledge that God had ordained her condition (v. 2; cf. Psa. 113:9). So she responded as any other woman in her time and circumstance would: she suggested Abraham take Sarah's servant, Hagar, and conceive a child for Sarah through her.

To accuse Sarah and Abraham of sexual immorality is a bit problematic. For one thing, Abraham did marry Hagar (v. 3). But it was also the norm in that time for a barren wife to provide her husband with a surrogate wife or concubine to produce children. So common was this reality that several legal codes sought to regulate it and its inevitable fallout. Other options included divorcing the first wife and marrying a more fertile woman, but this was not economically ideal because a divorced woman took the bride price and her dowry with her. It was thus considered preferable for a barren wife to provide a surrogate for her husband. If what Sarah had in mind was consistent with the custom of the day, Sarah would have had a legal prerogative to consider any child born to Hagar as her own (v. 2; cf. 30:6, 20).

And if this were a secular story, this plan would be all well and good. But Abraham's (and Sarah's) story is a spiritual one about how wide life's pendulum can swing between faith and fear.

Throughout the narrative, Abraham's passivity stands in stark contrast to the valiant warrior who attacked Chedorlaomer's forces with tenacity and daring. He now seems resigned to the whims of his wife and reluctant to get involved with the subsequent fallout.

Abraham's lack of leadership in his own home is disconcerting. Here, as before Pharaoh, the patriarch is hardly the father of the faithful. No better is Sarah, who clearly knew her barrenness was the Lord's doing, but inexplicably opted not to turn to prayer and petition for a reversal of her condition. That she did what culture expected is no excuse. Hers cannot be a model for us to follow. This is another immutable principle of the life of faith: what culture tolerates and God demands are often worlds apart.

Vivid language describes the dynamic between Sarah and Hagar. The text says that her maidservant treated her master "with contempt," the same Hebrew word used in 12:3 when God promised to curse those who dishonored Abraham. The Law of Moses demanded the death penalty for children who cursed their parents (Exod. 21:17; Lev. 20:9). Yet here we have Hagar, Abraham's new wife, dishonoring his first wife!

Sarah was livid at Hagar's disrespect and was likely overly dramatic, but when Abraham refused to get involved, she started treating her servant "harshly." We can scarcely blame Hagar, then, for fleeing from such a terrible situation in the direction of her homeland. Notwithstanding the fact that she had brought some of it on herself by treating Sarah as she did, the picture of an expectant mother alone in the desert arouses tremendous sympathy in the reader. Hagar is vulnerable and no doubt feels betrayed and abandoned.

Despondent in the desert, Hagar encountered divine intervention. We can become so entangled with trying to figure out the exact identity of "the angel of the LORD" that we miss the tenderness and care God exhibited towards Hagar. Abraham and Sarah had only referred to Hagar as "my/your servant," but God is the first in the narrative to call Hagar by her own name. To the Lord, she was so much more than a servant; by calling her name, God expressed the great value he had placed on her. As vulnerable and alone as she might have felt, Hagar had captured God's concern. Remarkably, he ushered her under the umbrella of the promise made to Abraham (v. 10).

It was at this point that Hagar realized she wasn't alone after all. God was not powerless; he was in control of everything. He was aware of her suffering, of her despair, of her impending pregnancy. He had already named her child and ordained a future for him. Hagar's story was not ending; it was only beginning. Hagar therefore called her mysterious messenger "a God who sees" (v. 13).

Hagar gave birth, and eleven years after leaving Haran, Abraham finally had a son. But it had come through human scheming, not the Lord's will. The end of the chapter leaves us with a startling dichotomy. It is Hagar, not Abraham and Sarah, who responded with faithful surrender to the Lord's will. If Abraham and Sarah had reacted to their own despair with something approaching Hagar's faith, the present crisis would have been averted, and this story would have turned out very differently. As it stands, the last 4,000 years are stained with the blood of Isaac's and Ishmael's descendants.

Read Genesis 17. Some thirteen years after Ishmael's birth, God again appeared to Abraham. Just as was noted in the first lesson, bestowing a name implied ownership and sovereignty in ancient times. But at the same time, a name-change said something about the destiny of the individual. Here, the Lord reaffirmed his previous promise to make the patriarch into a large nation (12:2; 13:16). And so sure was that promise that God altered Abram's name to *Abraham*; the former meant "exalted father," while the new name meant "father of many." To the previous promise of becoming a nation came the added vow "kings shall come from you" (17:6), and God promised to perpetuate the covenant to successive generations.

God also made this promise: "I will give to you and to your offspring after you the land of your sojournings, all the land of Canaan, for an everlasting possession, and I will be their God" (17:8).

God's gift of land to Abraham's posterity (Israel) was conditional on the Lord remaining their God. If Israel rebelled against him, all bets were off. Both Lev. 26 and Deut. 28 enumerate certain covenant curses to be brought on Israel if she did not keep the Law, and a very prominent one is expulsion from the land.

The sign of this Abrahamic covenant would be circumcision, a well-attested practice in ancient times, so it would not have been a new idea to Abraham—of all the nations appearing in the Old Testament, only the Philistines are known as the "uncircumcised" (Judg. 15:18; 1 Sam. 17:26, 36). Egyptian literature from the 22nd century speaks of circumcision, and a scene from inside a tomb depicting a circumcision ritual may be older than that. But while circumcision was practiced for a wide variety of reasons in ancient times, it was most often a rite of passage into purity, puberty, adulthood, or marriage. So what meaning did it have for ancient Israel in light of God's covenant with their father Abraham?

Notice that, going forward, every male born to Abraham's covenant lineage was to be circumcised, as well as every male bought as a slave (v. 12). It was to be a "sign" of the covenant, one by which God and man are both reminded of their obligations and promises under the Abrahamic covenant. God sees circumcision and is reminded of his oath to multiply the patriarch greatly. Man sees circumcision and is reminded of his obligation to trust in the promises and providence of God. For national Israel, this would be critically important since they would dwell in a Canaan's land plagued by pagan fertility cults. It was not Baal whom they should trust to bless them with children, but in the God of their fathers.

For the first time, Abraham's wife Sarah is made an explicit party to the covenant between God and the patriarch. The son of Abraham and Hagar is not the child of promise, for God's covenant is not with Abraham and Hagar, but with Abraham and Sarah—a new name that carried with it a renewed hope! Unlike Abraham's name, *Sarai* and *Sarah* are essentially the same—both mean "princess." But while the meaning of her name may not have changed, Sarah now has the assurance that her God is aware of her barrenness, and that his covenant with Abraham also holds just as much hope for her.

It's easy to forget that for the past thirteen years, Abraham had been living under the assumption that Ishmael was the fulfillment of the promise of posterity. So it must have been odd for the patriarch to hear God again promise a son, and no less through Sarah. Abraham begged, "Oh that Ishmael might live before you!" (17:18), meaning "Why not let Ishmael inherit what you have promised me?"

"No, Abraham," God says. No, Ishmael would not be the child of promise, for this is not what God had planned. The Lord had a specific will in this matter, and no plan or purpose of his can be thwarted. Ishmael would receive God's blessing (v. 20), and God kept every promise made here concerning Ishmael. But the oldest son of Abraham would not inherit the covenant. That privilege was reserved for Isaac ("he laughs"), one whose very birth and existence was met with skepticism, incredulity, and laughter. This was a sovereign decision on God's part. Note that this choice had nothing to do with Ishmael's or Isaac's salvation. The Lord was not predestinating one for eternal bliss or suffering. Rather, this choice had to do with membership in the covenant community of Israel and placement in the lineage that would culminate in the Incarnation of God's special Son, one that would be likened to Isaac.

And as if to signal that this topic was no longer open to additional debate, God abruptly left (v. 22). The patriarch's response is as commendable as was Noah's (6:22; 7:5). Abraham saw to it that he, his son Ishmael, and all the males in his house were circumcised. The narrator takes up five verses to assert redundantly that this was done "as God had said."

APPLICATION

Running Ahead of God. It is sometimes necessary that we be proactive in our Christian lives. God does not intend for us to be Christian couch potatoes waiting for the Lord's return. We must at times, as my dad often put it, "put legs on our prayers." But for all the times when we fail to act when we should, we just as often jump the gun, run ahead of God, and make a mess of things when we should have waited on him. Countless times in Scripture, God's people acted when they should have waited. Abraham and Sarah are perfect examples. Even with the noble purpose of "trying to help God out" by giving Hagar to Abraham, the fact remains that they acted outside of God's will. Christians must, therefore, be sensitive to God's guidance at certain times. Surely there are times when we much act instead of doing nothing, but we just as often are called to wait upon the Lord, to learn patience, and to await the arrival of God's perfect timing. Praying for patience and wisdom can surely aid us in remaining faithful during these painfully ambiguous seasons of life.

The Disenfranchised. Floundering in the undercurrent of Sarah's mistreatment of Hagar is a biblical principle concerning how we (mis)treat the disenfranchised of society. In the Law, God was clear that his people were to show kindness to, and maintain justice for, the down-and-out—the orphan, the widow, and the immigrant (Deut. 16:11; 24:17; 26:12; 27:19). Israel's obligation in this matter was derived from God's identity as a "father of the fatherless and protector of widows" (Psa. 68:5). When the Lord indignantly enumerated through the prophets the covenant failures of his people, social injustice always held a prominent place (Jer. 22:3; Ezek. 22:7; Zech. 7:10; Mal 3:5). This ethic is preserved in the New Testament, where we are commanded to "visit" (Jas. 1:27) or "look after" orphans and widows. If our concern for these individuals wanes, we lose out on seeing Jesus at work in our world, and our hearts grow calloused towards those who have much to teach us about daily reliance on the Father.

Seal of Circumcision. Wedding rings are a symbol of the marriage covenant made between a man and woman. Likewise, circumcision was a symbol of the covenant God made with Abraham, and the Lord ordained that it be practiced in the future so that his people would carry a reminder that the Lord was their God, a God of promises and provision. Circumcision was an affirmation of faith in this God. However, Israel eventually put too much stock in circumcision and too little in their faith. It became an empty ritual. In the New Testament, the apostle Paul drew parallels between Jewish circumcision and "the circumcision of Christ" (Col. 2:11–13). The sign of the covenant for Christians is no longer something done in the flesh, but an event from 2,000 years ago: the crucifixion and resurrection of Jesus that is reenacted in baptism. We are buried with him in water and raised as a new creature (2 Cor. 5:17) by God's matchless power. Like a wedding ring, our baptism is a reminder of God's oath to declare us "not guilty" before his judgment seat on the final day (Rom. 8:1).

CONCLUSION

It was wrong for Abraham and Sarah to attempt to circumvent God's plan or to "help him out." It was also wrong for Sarah and Hagar to treat one another so spitefully. But God cared for all of them, and that is why he was faithful to them in spite of their sin. God does not even allow human frailty and failure to stand in the way of his purposes for his people. He is faithful when we are faithless. His plan for Israel, to say nothing of Christ, was still on track. And as circumcision did for Abraham, our baptism reminds us that God's plan will continue abated until the end of time. "He who began a good work in you will bring it to completion at the day of Jesus Christ" (Phil. 1:6).

QUESTIONS FOR REFLECTION

1. What options did a barren woman like Sarah have to provide her husband with a child? Why were none of these options advisable for a person of faith like Sarah?

2. Is Abraham portrayed as active or passive in Gen. 16?

3. How did God express his concern and care for Hagar?

4. What did the seal of circumcision represent? How did it remind both God and man of their covenant responsibilities?

5. Describe the differences (if any) between Abraham's and Sarah's old/new names.

6. What protest did Abraham offer up to the new covenant and why?

QUESTIONS FOR DISCUSSION

1. Have you ever been mistreated by someone else? How did God remind you of his care and concern during that difficult time?

2. Why is it so important to "visit" or "look out for" the disenfranchised of society?

3. In what ways have you been guilty of "running ahead of God" and trying to help him out in an unauthorized way?

4. How has God reaffirmed his grace to you in the aftermath?

5. In the age of Christ, what is the replacement for circumcision? Of what is it intended to remind us?

9

A PROMISED SON

GENESIS 18

Objective: To emphasize how God is more powerful and loving than we can imagine

INTRODUCTION

Nearly a quarter of a century had passed since God had made Abraham the promise to make his name great. That promise had been further specified that he would receive a child from his loins, and that he would become the father of many nations through a child born to him via Sarah. But no such child had been conceived.

In this story, God arrives for a visit in mysterious form. So imagine the patriarch's shock (let alone Sarah's) when the "visitor" informed them that they would have a son within a year! Later, God decided to inform Abraham of his plan to destroy Sodom. By considering these two episodes in this chapter—one very happy and the other very sad—we discover that God is both more powerful and more gracious than we could ever imagine.

EXAMINATION

Read Genesis 18:1-15. While Abraham was still residing in Hebron, God visited him, accompanied by two companions, in the middle of the day. The time of the visit is given for more than just a time-stamp. Per the custom of the day, the patriarch was likely preparing for an afternoon nap. But when he saw that he had company, Abraham dispensed with his personal agenda and welcomed these three travelers. There also may be unique significance in Abraham's running and bowing; elsewhere in Genesis, people only run to greet long-lost relatives (29:13; 33:4), and only bow in the presence of the powerful (37:9; 42:6).

Abraham certainly displayed impressive hospitality by summoning bread (something resembling pita bread), curds of yogurt, goat's milk (highly valued in ancient times), and a choice roasted calf from his herd. The patriarch's generosity is heightened by the terms "went quickly" and "ran" (vv. 6-7). He went to great and urgent lengths to care for the needs of his guests.

During the meal, God asked, "Where is Sarah your wife?" a question to which God already knew the answer. It is here that Old Testament scholar John H. Walton makes an interesting observation. He wonders why the three guests would inquire as to Sarah's whereabouts. If these visitors were supernatural and omniscient beings (and they were), the question was unnecessary unless the Lord was calling attention to something that was out-of-sorts (and he was).

Walton contends it was not the practice of that time for women to eat separately from men, so Sarah might have confined herself to the tent because she had begun menstruating (cf. 31:34–35). At some point during the meal, Sarah became understandably alarmed when she began menstruating, something that should not have happened given her age (v. 11). Walton thus asserts that the arrival of these three visitors triggered "the resumption of her fertility."

Walton's suggestion is as plausible as it is outlandish, but we must not get so consumed with why Sarah was in the tent that we miss the subsequent scene. God specifically promised Abraham and Sarah that they would have a son within the year. The absurd thought of Sarah conceiving is expressed with the phrase, "The way of women had ceased to be with Sarah" (v. 11), a reference to female menstruation. Most modern translations delicately gloss over the phrase with something like "Sarah was past the age of childbearing" (NIV), but I prefer the literal translation. The entire scene rudely calls attention to the fact that Sarah's pregnancy would not be confused as being ordinary or natural.

Even more complicating is Sarah's retort that she and Abraham were old, and her rhetorical question, "Shall I have pleasure?" may indicate they had stopped having intercourse. The narrator certainly went overboard in highlighting Abraham's and Sarah's ages; he says they "were old, advanced in years" (v. 11), and quotes Sarah as saying that she is "worn out" and her husband is "old" (v. 12). How was she to conceive when the complications of aging presented too much of a hurdle? The answer is that nothing is too hard for God (v. 14)!

Read Genesis 18:16-33. As hospitality of the time dictated, when the three travelers arose to leave, Abraham journeyed with them to "see them off," and they came to a place where Sodom and Gomorrah could be seen. There and then, God decided to inform Abraham of the possible fate of these cities.

In what follows, we are presented with an odd, seemingly incomprehensible, scene in which the patriarch presumed to test the boundaries of the Lord. Abraham could not conceive how a righteous God, which he perceived God to be, could throw a moral baby out with the immoral bathwater. "Far be it from you to do such a thing, to put the righteous to death with the wicked, so that the righteous fare as the wicked! Far be that from you! Shall not the Judge of all the earth do what is just?" (v. 25). So Abraham haggled with God, and what the patriarch learned has the ability to change the world.

Old Testament scholar Nathan MacDonald provides us with an excellent summation of the haggling process so common in Middle Eastern culture: "The technical rules of haggling are essentially universal. The buyer approaches the vendor, who gives the initial price; bids then alternate between the two and converge. If complete convergence is reached, the sale is consummated. In the haggle, backward moves are forbidden and accepted bids must be honored."

MacDonald goes on to point out that, given this description, Abraham clearly entered into the discussion thinking it to be a haggling situation. He would ask for fifty souls and expected God to counter with a higher number—say, 100?—at which point Abraham would counter the counter-offer until the two parties met somewhere in the middle. In other words, I think Abraham believed it was his responsibility to soften the stance of a trigger-happy, overly-vengeful God, to invite "the Judge of all the earth" to be more reasonable.

What he discovered, instead, is that God has a greater capacity for mercy than we can imagine. Yes, his justice is above our own, but so is his mercy. At no point in the conversation did God ever counter-offer Abraham, so the patriarch kept on going, eventually stopping with a deal in which Sodom would be spared if ten righteous souls were found. Why ten? MacDonald suggests Abraham may have stopped at ten, not because God somehow signaled that the limit was being reached, but because Abraham was confused or embarrassed at being able to go so far below his original "asking price"—something that would have never happened while haggling in the marketplace. If you offer to buy a piece of fruit for $1, you can abandon any hope of getting it for less—unless the person you're dealing with is infinitely benevolent.

Abraham entered into the negotiation believing that he would have to talk God into being more merciful, yet it was God who taught the patriarch that the mercy of the Lord is greater than we can comprehend. The patriarch was willing to see Sodom destroyed in spite of nine righteous souls. God, it seems, might have been willing to go lower. Couple that with God's unnecessary plan to go and investigate for himself the wickedness of the city, and we are given a glimpse at just how reluctant God was to destroy a city that became a by-word for utter wickedness.

APPLICATION

Power in Weakness. Throughout Scripture, the omnipotence and omniscience of God are often celebrated, but never more so than in 18:1-15. No sooner had he revealed his knowledge of Sarah's laughter than God asked, "Is anything too hard for the LORD?" At our lowest and most vulnerable, when we believe all hope is gone, we need reminding that God sees and knows our plight, and that he cares. We also need reminding that he is powerful enough to do something about our circumstances. As he often does with us, perhaps God intentionally delayed the fulfillment of his promise these many years until Abraham and Sarah were completely broken. He did so in order to teach them that the power and grace of God are never more matchless than when we believe things have passed the point of no return. Well did Jesus say that the poor in spirit, those so despondent in their soul, were qualified for citizenship in heaven's kingdom (Matt 5:3). It is only when we abandon our own agenda that we can see God's at work.

An Ordained End. It demands remarkable faith to believe that God has appointed an end to our suffering while we are suffering! But how thrilling it is that we are invited to believe the impossible! When he informed the couple that Isaac would be born within a year, God was ordaining an end to their barrenness in suffering. In like manner, God invites us to have faith that he is powerful enough to end our suffering, though we remain in our suffering. Our faith must thus be coupled with hope. In the midst of our disappointment and despair, God's sovereignty is the only appropriate basis for our hope. When our hearts become convinced that God can do all things—that he is patiently working out his plan in the world—we will find no command of his too arduous, and no promise too ridiculous.

Role of Fatherhood. In 18:19, it is obvious that God considered it Abraham's obligation to teach his posterity about the righteousness and justice of God, and this obligation belongs to every family patriarch. The problem is that the once exalted position of father has been drug through the mud in recent times. In TV sitcoms, fathers are often portrayed as incompetent, bumbling idiots. The mounting stack of studies heralding the necessity of strong, benevolent fathers in our society only repeats the earlier, necessary, clear and decisive biblical call for fatherhood. A father is responsible for teaching his children the will of God and reaffirming the faithfulness of God (Exod. 12:26–27; Deut. 6:6–7; Isa. 38:19). A father is responsible for loving and disciplining his children so that they might become men and women of God (Psa. 103:13; Prov. 3:12). It is admittedly a difficult balance to strike, the balance between love and fairness. But by praying to their heavenly Father and asking for his wisdom (cf. Jas. 1:5), today's fathers can, like Abraham, teach their children properly about the righteousness and justice of God.

CONCLUSION

There can be no question that ours is a holy and just God who must punish evil and wickedness. Throughout Genesis, it has already become apparent to us that God reaches his limit eventually and must execute wrath on evildoers (e.g. the Flood, Babel). But God is also more gracious than our finite minds can imagine. Seemingly, never in Abraham's wildest dreams did he believe the Judge of all the earth would settle for ten righteous souls in Sodom. Nor did he easily believe that God would give he and Sarah a son in their old age. But that's exactly what happened. This lesson, then, presents us with two things to celebrate as the people of God—that the Lord is more powerful than we can imagine and that he is more gracious than we can imagine.

QUESTIONS FOR REFLECTION

1. Why does the narrator tell us this event took place in the middle of the day?

2. What all did Abraham do to extend hospitality to his guests?

3. Why did God ask where Sarah was during the meal?

4. What does the narrator tell us to draw attention to Sarah's age?

5. Why did God decide to warn Abraham about the fate of Sodom?

6. What did Abraham expect to happen when he began haggling with God?

QUESTIONS FOR DISCUSSION

1. In your life, how exactly have you struggled to believe that nothing is impossible with God?

2. Why is it important to focus on the sovereignty of God in the midst disappointment and despair?

3. What example does Abraham set for today's father?

4. What do we learn about God's nature by his haggling with Abraham?

10

SODOM & GOMORRAH

GENESIS 19

Objective: To understand the sin of Sodom
and learn from the city's destruction

INTRODUCTION

The cities of Sodom and Gomorrah have become bywords in Christian circles for homosexuality, and justifiably so. In our own time, the homosexual community has made alarming strides in gaining recognition from various sectors of our culture. It should be deeply disturbing to any godly man or woman to see homosexuals being granted the right to marry, adopt children, etc.

But in these chapters, the righteous judgment and destruction of Sodom by a holy God underscore broader principles that we shall explore. Elsewhere in Scripture, we learn that showing hospitality is of great priority to the Lord, and a lack of it was among the reasons he destroyed these cities of the Plain. Hospitality flows from a heart that is saturated with compassion, even for those who do not love God or live lives that honor him.

There is a lesson there, I think, for the children of Abraham: we must love all those created in God's image, even homosexuals, and wish for them nothing less than a relationship with the One who wants to be their Savior before he becomes their Judge.

EXAMINATION

Read Genesis 19:1-29. If you look at a map of the Dead Sea, you will notice a peninsula jutting out from its southeastern bank; the Sea north of the peninsula is 1,300 feet deep in some places, but only 20 feet in depth south of this peninsula. It's possible that at one time this peninsula was the Dead Sea's southern shore, and that the shallow end of the Dead Sea now was previously the Valley of Siddim (14:3), the location of Sodom and her sister cities.

It has been noted in several places that the city gates in ancient times functioned as courthouses/town halls/community centers. Lot's presence at Sodom's city gates means he was considered a prominent member of the community, though his immigrant status was later thrown in his face (v. 9). Lot had risen in Sodom's society, and while it would spell his downfall, it doesn't seem to have ruined his good manners or hospitable spirit.

The two angels who had journeyed to Sodom were greeted by Lot upon arrival, and he extended to them courtesy similar to what Abraham had done: he offered to wash their feet and "made them a feast" including bread. Because it was already evening, social standards of hospitality dictated that he offer lodging, not just a simple meal. The angels initially refused Lot's offer, but he twisted their arm until they consented. Whether or not Lot knew their supernatural identity, he certainly knew about the immoral sexual desires of his neighbors, and he did not want his guests to be subjected to the violence of Sodom's men.

No sooner had Lot led his guests home but a mob formed outside his door. This wasn't limited to a few men. It was "all the people to the last man" (v. 4)—a phrase that creates serious doubt in the reader's mind that Abraham's ten righteous souls could actually be found in Sodom (18:32).

What did the mob want? Up until recently, it was universally acknowledged that their desires were not only immoral, but also unnatural. They wanted to have homosexual intercourse with Lot's guests. In more modern times, however, spectacularly vigorous attempts have been made to reinterpret the mob's (and by extension, Sodom's) sin, with suggestions ranging from a lack of hospitality to a violation of the rule of law.

But notice that the mob wanted to "know" Lot's visitors, and if Lot offered his daughters to the mob as an alternative—daughters "who have not known any man"—then are we seriously expected to conclude that the mob's original demand wasn't sexual? Arguably, Lot's offer to the mob to satisfy their lust with his virgin daughters is more disturbing than their previous request. His offer was ghastly, cowardly, and indefensible.

The mob began to wantonly beat the door down, seemingly intent on raping Lot instead of the angels. That's when the angels struck the mob with "blindness." The angels' act was supernaturally debilitating and disorienting. Yet so determined was this mob in its degenerate lust that they did not disperse; "they wore themselves out groping for the door" (v. 11).

Meanwhile, the urgency of the angels kicked in. They ordered Lot to gather up his family post-haste and get out of the city as quickly as possible. Lot implored his sons-in-law (since his daughters were still virgins, they were likely his sons-in-law to-be) to join him in leaving the city. But for whatever reason, Lot had zero influence on them. We are told that they thought he was "jesting" (v. 14)

Notice also the way Lot drug his feet and delayed in getting out of town. The text says Lot "lingered" (v. 16) or "hesitated" (HCSB), so much so that it seems God mercifully delayed the destruction until the angels had seized Lot and his family and almost drug them out of the city. And if that isn't enough, Lot whined that the distance he was expected to travel was too far (v. 20). In the face of the terrible, awesome judgment of God, only a fool dares delay his own salvation, and only a gracious God stalls his wrath until we have gotten out of our own way (cf. 2 Pet. 3:9).

I have always pictured Lot's wife looking back in the sense of glancing wistfully over her shoulder at the city (i.e. the life) she was leaving behind, and then poof! she became a pillar of salt. But there may have been more to it than that. In his comments in Luke 17:28-32, Jesus may suggest that she went so far as to return to the city. More than a knee-jerk glance over the shoulder; it evokes Lot's wife losing faith in her husband (and in God). But this decision on her part proved fatal. In the face of God's judgment, it is foolishness to continue to identify with the objects of our past affections.

How exactly was Sodom destroyed? The text says sulfur and fire rained down from heaven, a statement Jesus later corroborated (Luke 17:29). Scientifically, it is suggested that an earthquake "overthrew" (v. 25) natural gas and petroleum pocketed in the ground (cf. 14:10) and sent them skyward, only to be ignited by lightning and fall back to earth, giving the appearance of raining sulfur and fire from heaven. The whole Jordan Valley sits on the Syrian-African Rift, so an earthquake isn't out of the question. But trying to understand what physically happened can undermine our appreciation for what spiritually happened. From the Bible's perspective, God had had enough of Sodom's evil. Notice that:

1. The destruction was *God's work*—the divine name ap-

pears no fewer than three times in the destruction account (vv. 23-26).

2. The destruction was *warranted*—"the Judge of all the earth" always does what is right (18:25).

3. The destruction was *total*—for not even plant life survived the destruction (v. 25).

In the final scene of the devastation, we are again reminded of Abraham. He returned to where he had previously bartered with the Lord for Sodom's survival and was met with confirmation that not even ten righteous souls had been found. Only one question remained on his mind: Had Lot been spared?

Read Genesis 19:30-39. For whatever reason, Lot and his daughters were afraid to stay in Zoar (v. 30), and they left the village to live in a cave, even though they had rejected that option the night before. Because the devastation was so widespread, they may have assumed the entire world had been destroyed. This explains why Lot's daughters desperately intoxicated their father and conceived by him.

Regardless, there is no denying that their desires were reprehensible, even by ancient standards. The phrase "lie with" is not as innocent as it sounds; it is used elsewhere in Genesis for other illicit sexual relationships (cf. 26:10; 34:2; 35:22; 39:7). And in spite of what some have suggested, there is absolutely no salvageable nobility in the daughters trying to secure an heir. That they had to get their own father drunk to accomplish their goal proves they knew their actions to be morally abhorrent. On the other hand, no blame for what transpired is assigned to Lot; the narrator stresses he was completely unaware of what happened.

The two sons born to Lot's daughters were named *Moab*, meaning "from my father," and *Ben-ammi*, meaning "son of my family."

Both became nations with whom Israel had occasional (often violent) contact, and while God prohibited their extermination (Deut. 2:9, 19), they nonetheless lived under his rejection (Deut. 23:3-6), though not forever (Jer. 48:47; 49:6).

APPLICATION

The Sin of Homosexuality. Though Sodom's sin was not limited to homosexuality, it is clear that its practice was a significant contributing factor to the city's destruction since this was the desire of the mob in the story. The New Testament certainly remembers Sodom as a den of sexual immorality (Jude 7). Elsewhere in the New Testament, Paul condemned the practice of homosexuality as unnatural and against God's will (Rom. 1:26-27). In 1 Cor. 6:9-10, he says plainly that sinners, including "the sexually immoral [...] nor men who practice homosexuality [...] will inherit the kingdom of God." Though it is becoming increasingly unpopular to maintain this view, Christians must be fiercely bold and lovingly courageous in condemning homosexuality as a practice that saddens the heart of God, lest Sodom and Gomorrah rise at the Judgment to condemn this generation.

Lordship of Jesus. Among the Millennial generation, there is a declining commitment to a biblical definition of sexuality and marriage. That trend should give us pause because it is the duty of every professed Christian to preserve and proclaim God's values to the world (Matt. 5:13-16). But on the other side of the equation are Christians who pretend that homosexuality is the worst sin imaginable. Is it? Jesus said that those who rejected both his messengers (Matt. 10:15) and his message (Matt. 11:24) would be in worse shape at the Judgment than the citizens of Sodom. Consider that claim. As utterly immoral as homosexuality is, Jesus considered it a graver sin to witness his works yet reject his Lordship. For the church, those for whom Christ has done marvelous things, Jesus' words mandate that we make him Lord of our whole lives. Explaining away his difficult teachings (e.g. discipleship, service, sacrificial love, radical obedience, divorce and remarriage) in order to soothe our guilty consciences is a practice the church should renounce with bitter tears. Otherwise, Sodom will fare better on the final day than we will. That fact alone should truly give us pause.

The Legacy of Lot. Lot is indeed a tragic character in Scripture. Once a very wealthy man, all that he owns in life can now fit inside a small cave. For all we know, this is his existence until death. But this should not come as a surprise to us. For too long, Lot had lived by his own self-sufficiency instead of an abiding faith in God. Earlier in the chapter, he had been willing to offer up his daughters to be gang-raped by the lustful mob in order to secure his own safety. He was revered as a spiritual leader by absolutely no one. It should be expected, then, that his daughters would lose all respect for him and resort to tricks, not trust, to meet their needs. It is a truth of Scripture that the sins of the parents fester and spread to successive generations. In the case of Lot, his (grand)sons spawned nations that were never known (not surprisingly) for their morality or righteousness. "Heavenly Father, give us more parents who set for their children a powerful example of what it means to trust and obey you in all things."

DIGGING DEEPER

Sodom's Sin. The cities of Sodom and Gomorrah, as previously mentioned, have in the Christian community become bywords for homosexuality. It's hard to reinterpret the demands and desires of the mob at Lot's door (v. 5).

But contrary to popular belief, homosexuality was not the sole reason for these cities' destruction. A very thorough illustration of Sodom's legacy is in Ezekiel. "This was the sin of your sister Sodom:

She and her daughters were proud and had plenty of food and lived in great comfort, but she did not help the poor and needy" (Ezek. 16:49 NCV). In addition to homosexuality and sexual immorality, pride and a systematic disregard for the less fortunate were also a part of Sodom's sin.

The cities of this area evidently enjoyed great wealth gained from very little work—note the allegation in Ezek. 16:49 of "idleness" (NKJV) or "careless ease" (NASU). The region was rich in a wide variety of natural resources. Sodom likely forced slaves to mine those minerals, then sat back as the lucrative profits rolled in. And if you're ridiculously wealthy, you're likely less inclined to share what you have with those in need.

Jewish legend preserved stories of Sodom's cruel lack of hospitality towards travelers and the poor. For example, when a beggar once appeared in Sodom, the city prohibited anyone from feeding him, hoping he would die of starvation. One woman had pity on him and would sneak him bread in the bottom of her water pitcher as she went to the city well each day. When the city leaders couldn't understand how the beggar kept on living, they stationed three men on a stakeout. They caught the woman red-handed and burned her alive.

I concede these stories may have been somewhat embellished over the years, but they nonetheless paint a picture of Sodom that is wholly consistent with the Scriptures. The reality is that the Sodomites weren't just considered sinners, but "wicked, great sinners against the LORD" (13:13). God brought judgment upon them, and our inability to even find their ruins today foreshadows the eternal fate of all the wicked.

But lest we think that such a fate only awaits homosexuals, or those who practice other forms of sexual immorality, we must know that this fearful retribution also awaits those void of compassion for the less fortunate. In the judgment scene of Matt. 25, Jesus says those who failed to show generosity to the needy will be banished from his presence and placed under God's eternal curse (Matt. 25:41). There is more to the life of faith than avoiding carnal lust or supporting a biblical definition of marriage. We must learn to regard all others as precious souls made in God's image. This was a pursuit at which Sodom failed miserably.

CONCLUSION

It is natural to wonder why Moses would record the story of Sodom's (and Lot's) demise. The final narrative of Gen. 19 does explain the origins of the Moabites and Ammonites, something Genesis is always interested in doing. But I believe Moses' greater motive was to prompt the reader to contrast the fates of Lot and Abraham. Lot is never mentioned again in Genesis, as the spotlight will now return to Abraham.

We are thus left with the stark realization of what it means to live by faith vs. by natural instinct. Lot chose the best land, established himself in a city, and had only war and destruction to show for it, living out the rest of his existence in a nameless cave. On the other hand, Abraham chose the land God had promised, continued to live in temporary dwellings, and despite his hiccups of faith, eventually "died at a ripe old age, old and contented" (Gen. 25:8 HCSB). The patriarch thus stands as an example of one who eschewed this world and its pleasures in exchange for the glories of endless fellowship with God (1 John 2:17).

QUESTIONS FOR REFLECTION

1. What does it say about Lot that he was at Sodom's city gates?

2. How is Abraham's hospitality in Gen. 18 and Lot's in this chapter compared and contrasted?

3. How do we know the mob's request was sexual in nature?

4. Was Lot reluctant to leave Sodom? How so? Why?

5. What was entailed in Lot's wife looking back at the city?

6. What motive did Lot's daughters have in wanting to conceive children by him?

7. What two nations came from this incestuous union?

QUESTIONS FOR DISCUSSION

1. Why is important to acknowledge that Sodom's sin was not *limited* to homosexuality?

2. How can Christians be sexually pure/moral, but still be guilty of Sodom's sin?

3. In what ways did Lot prove himself to be a poor spiritual leader?

4. As he did for Lot, in what ways has God forestalled his wrath until you got out of your own way?

5. What does this statement mean to you: "In the face of God's judgment, it is foolishness to continue to identify with the objects of our past affections"?

6. What are common objections given to the Bible's condemnation of homosexuality?

11

ABRAHAM & ISAAC

GENESIS 21-22

Objective: To affirm that God faithfully
provides for all those who trust Him

INTRODUCTION

For a quarter of a century, Abraham struggled to trust consistently in God's promises. But a year after God visited Abraham, he visited Sarah in a different way, and the promise of a son was actualized. Imagine, then, the agony in Abraham's heart as he faced the prospect of sacrificing his son to God, just as he had been instructed to do. The test of Abraham's faith on Mt. Moriah was no less significant than Isaac's birth, and it proved to be the pivotal moment of the patriarch's life. The story illustrates the purest and most mature expression of faith and obedience possible. Not only does the odyssey of faith have its twists and turns, but also its own agonizing moments on the mountaintop and the valley below. Through it all, our trust and confidence in God is being strengthened, as was father Abraham's.

EXAMINATION

Read Genesis 21. God is faithful. As he has done on countless occasions throughout history, he remembered the despair of one in a hopeless situation. Sarah gave birth to a son, and he was given a name precisely as God had promised (17:19). This birth took place at the appointed time (v. 2); God had appointed an end to this couple's suffering, and the Lord had been faithful!

The narrator artfully underscores the event's absurdity by noting both Abraham's and Sarah's shock over having a child at such an advanced age (vv. 5-7). There is much ado made over their elderly state—not out of rudeness, but in an effort to celebrate the unparalleled power of God. But the joy over Isaac's birth was shattered a few years later by another family feud. During a celebration commemorating Isaac's weaning, Ishmael was caught doing something (v. 9), and we presume that it was directed at Isaac.

Whatever the crime, it was enough to infuriate Sarah—she never even mentions Ishmael or Hagar by name, and she demanded that Abraham divorce Hagar and banish her and her son from the family. Abraham, for understandable reasons, was not so easily inclined to do so to satisfy the wrath of his first wife. The text says Sarah's demand was "displeasing" (v. 11) to Abraham, but God gave assurances of his providence for Hagar and Ishmael.

As God had commanded, Abraham outfitted Hagar and Ishmael for their departure, but their provisions were rather sparse for a multiday journey into the desert; the skin of water given to Hagar held no more than three gallons and would have only lasted them a few days. When it was gone, Hagar and Ishmael despondently resigned themselves to death. But God graciously heard their prayer, their cry for help. The Lord had promised Abraham that Ishmael would become a nation. The promise was reiterated here to Hagar, and we know that when God ordains a future, he also meets the needs of the present. Hagar's eyes were opened to a well that would quench their thirst.

Before moving on to the next passage, take just a moment to read and ponder the startling statement, "God was with the boy" (v. 20). The passage is clear that Ishmael was not a part of the plan, the one that commenced with Abraham and would culminate with the Incarnation—for such an honor was reserved for Isaac. But that doesn't mean Ishmael was cast from the divine presence and made to live outside of God's favor. Rather, it may be that the Lord established Ishmael as the patriarch of his own nation in order to make up for the inheritance Ishmael lost when he was cast from Abraham's house and effectively written out of the will.

Not too long after Hagar and Ishmael departed, Abraham was visited by Abimelech and Phicol, respectively the king and military commander of Gerar. The treaty they sought would not only be with the patriarch, but also with his God. The reason he wanted the patriarch to "swear" is precisely because Abraham had been deceptive previously during their prior engagement in Gen. 20. Simply put, Abimelech did not trust Abraham.

But if the patriarch was going to consent to this pact of non-aggression, then he also wanted to raise concerns when his rights were violated. Moses says "Abraham reproved Abimelech about a well of water that Abimelech's servants had seized," and according to one scholar, "the Hebrew verb suggests that Abraham had to make his complaint several times."

In an arid region such as the one Abraham inhabited on this occasion, one that may have averaged only a foot of rain per annum, wells were quite valuable. What Abimelech's servants were doing was essentially stealing. In response to Abraham's complaint, Abimelech claimed he had no knowledge of the act. Abraham took sheep and oxen with which the two men "cut a covenant," likely in a way similar to that of

Gen. 15. But the patriarch also took seven ewe lambs as an additional witness that the well was his. The well was given the name "Beersheba," a word that can mean both "well of seven" and "well of oaths."

Read Genesis 22. To this point, Abraham has run the gamut of spiritual maturity in the past four decades or so. He has endured many highs and lows. He was willing to displace his family from their homeland, but unwilling to be honest about his marriage. He was willing to attack superior enemy forces, but cowered before kings and subjected himself to his wife's occasional whims. Always at stake on these occasions was the question: "Does Abraham trust God to provide?"

The narrative opens by telling us that God intended to test Abraham. Opening the passage this way teaches us that God was testing the patriarch, and thus should shift our focus away from our concern for Isaac's life to concern for Abraham's faith. Too often, a newcomer reads the text, wondering, "Oh no! Does Isaac survive?" when it should be asked, "Oh no! Will Abraham obey?" Even in the worst-case scenario, sincere faith is more valuable than long life in God's economy (Matt. 16:25).

The Lord made an inconceivable request of Abraham. "Take your son, your only son Isaac, whom you love, and go to the land of Moriah, and offer him there as a burnt offering on one of the mountains of which I shall tell you" (v. 2). The enormity of what God was asking of Abraham is underscored by the triple designation of his son: "your son, your only son, whom you love—Isaac."

Isaac's designation as Abraham's "only son" should arrest our attention and give us pause. The prophets Jeremiah and Amos used the phrase "mourning as for an only son" as a euphemism for the deepest expression of grief. The death of an only son wasn't just the death of a beloved child, but "the end of the family line," and was thus considered "a terrible catastrophe." Abraham had loved Ishmael and been quite reluctant to dismiss him. How much more so would Isaac's certain doom be the capstone on his life of grief? Surely this was too much for God to ask of the patriarch. But Abraham realized that only when we have surrendered what is most valuable to us, making God the sole Author of our story, can we fully experience the glory of life with the Lord.

As the fateful party neared Moriah, the narrator intentionally slows the pace of the storytelling. He does this that we might reflect on how grave an act Abraham is about to commit, and one borne of his faith in God. An affectionate father is about to sacrifice the life of his so-very-special son. Once on the mountain, Abraham and his son went about preparing the sacrifice. We would have to conclude that Isaac was quite dense if we assume he was unaware of his role in this drama. He seems to have willingly allowed himself to be bound and placed upon the altar. And here we have a startling picture of Abraham prepared not simply to stab his son and then walk away to be alone in his grief. No, he is prepared to "slaughter" (v. 10) his son as one would a sacrificial animal—to disembowel Isaac as if he were an ox from Abraham's herd. Such is the depth of the patriarch's commitment to obey his God.

But then Abraham heard a voice, and a most blessed one. It was the same voice that had commanded him to make this journey. It now ordered him to stand down. And just as that voice spoke, a sacrificial ram caught Abraham's eye. There would be a sacrifice offered this day, but it would be a substitutionary one. So overwhelmed was he with this turn of events that Abraham marked this mountain with the Hebrew words *yhwh yireh*—"Yahweh will provide."

The final few verses of the chapter concern the growth of Abraham's extended family. They have not been mentioned since Abraham left them behind in Haran at the beginning of Gen. 12. But here he receives word that his brother Nahor had been blessed with a dozen sons. Among them was Bethuel, who had fathered a daughter, Rebekah. The stage is thus set for a transition from Abraham's life to Isaac's. But first, a requiem…

APPLICATION

You Didn't Build That. In 2012, President Obama elicited a backlash when he told an audience: "If you've got a business—you didn't build that. Somebody else made that happen." The words "You didn't build that" quickly went viral on social media. I don't believe that government deserves much credit for the success of hard-working people. But neither do I believe that hard-working people deserve much credit for the success of hard-working people. Biblical faith demands we acknowledge God as the source of all blessings (Jas. 1:17). The text makes abundantly clear how ridiculous it would be to suggest Isaac's conception was a natural event. He was unequivocally God's blessing to Abraham and Sarah. And since God was the Author of Isaac's life, Abraham believed he could sacrifice Isaac at God's command, convinced "that God was able even to raise him from the dead" (Heb. 11:19). If you are having difficulty surrendering to God what is most valuable to you, perhaps you have never acknowledged it as coming from him to begin with. But when you come to the place where your faith allows you to withhold nothing, your eyes are then opened to see the glorious things God can do with your life.

Provision for the Future. Alone, despondent, starving and thirsty in the desert—this is the state we find Hagar and Ishmael. In his great mercy, God gave Hagar a glimpse into the future at the things he had prepared for her son. And when God ordains a future, he also meets the needs of the present. A well was revealed to Hagar, and her needs were met. Though we are not promised a certain length of life on earth, God has ordained the impregnability of the church against the forces of Satan, as well as the surety of his commitment to his own glory. Thus, Christians can have peace that God is in control, his church will continue, and that God will continue to glorify himself no matter what. Sometimes it requires great faith to trust in these promises, for the "evidence" says otherwise. But Christians walk by faith, not sight (2 Cor. 5:7). Therefore, just as we are to be unwavering in trusting God's ordained future, we must also be unwavering in obeying his commands and looking to him for provision.

Faith Is the Victory. The history of Christianity is filled with the names of brave martyrs who willingly gave up their lives rather than renounce their faith. The reason they did so is because they understood that, in God's economy, sincere faith is more valuable than long life. Though most of us will likely never be called to renounce Christ or die, we are daily placed in situations and circumstances where we are tempted to take the reasonable path of the world vs. the ill-advised, risky path that faith demands. In many ways, faith is often at odds with common sense. Wisdom in Scripture is always oriented around the principle of fearing the Lord (Prov. 1:7). We must understand that the most important question in life is not "How do I live the longest life or the best life?" but "Will I trust and obey God?

CONCLUSION

The significance of Isaac's birth does not go unnoticed in the New Testament. One writer referred to Isaac as Abraham's "only begotten son" (Heb. 11:17 NKJV), a phrase used elsewhere only of Jesus (cf. John 1:14; 3:16). But this designation is not the only parallel between Isaac and Jesus. In many ways, Isaac embodied all the promises God had made to Abraham, and Christ certainly embodies the same for us—in him is our hope for forgiveness (Eph. 4:32) and a verdict of "not guilty" (Rom. 8:1). He is our hope for an abundant life here on earth (John 10:10) and an eternal one in heaven (Rom. 6:23). Indeed, the most mature expression of our reliance on God would be to trust in the promise of Phil. 4:19—"My God will supply every need of yours according to his riches in glory in Christ Jesus."

QUESTIONS FOR REFLECTION

1. How does the narrator express shock at Abraham's and Sarah's advanced age when Isaac was born?

2. How did God provide for Hagar and Ishmael in the desert?

3. What question drives the story of Abraham's life? What question should we ask ourselves as the story unfolds?

4. Why does the text remind us that Isaac was Abraham's "only son" (22:2)?

5. What name did Abraham give the mountain at the end of the story? What is the significance of the name?

QUESTIONS FOR DISCUSSION

1. What does this statement mean to you: "When God ordains a future, he also meets the needs of the present"?

2. What does this statement mean to you: "In God's economy, sincere faith is more valuable than long life"?

3. In what ways have you struggled to believe that God will provide?

4. Why is it important to acknowledge God as the source of every blessing?

5. In what ways has God proven himself faithful in providing for your needs and keeping his promises?

6. How does Christ, like Isaac, embody all the promises of God? What New Testament passages speak to this?

12

A FUNERAL & A WEDDING

GENESIS 23-24

Objective: To see how Abraham trusted God
in burying Sarah and seeking a wife for Isaac

INTRODUCTION

So far in Genesis, the focus has been primarily on the story of
Abraham. But as the life of the patriarch is winding down, the covenant promises are about to pass to the next generation. We witness the
death of Sarah, and as any parent can relate, the reader is confronted
with several questions at this juncture. Will God be as faithful to
Isaac as he had been to Abraham? Will Isaac enjoy as many covenant
blessings as his father? And what of Isaac's relationship with God?
Will he be as faithful as his father? What if he does not marry well?
Will the immoral influence of the neighboring Canaanites consume
this unique heir of Abraham as it had Lot, the patriarch's nephew?
This section of Genesis narrates how God's plan continued to unfold
within the covenant family.

EXAMINATION

Read Genesis 23. Sarah is the only woman in Scripture whose life span is given at her death: 127 years. When she passed away at Kiriath-arba, the text says Abraham mourned and wept for her. Biblical customs concerning grief entailed various combinations of fasting, tearing of garments, disheveling or shaving one's hair or beard, throwing dirt on the head, and sitting in ashes. Abraham no doubt engaged in at least some, if not all, of these practices in order to mark his beloved's passing.

It was then that he approached the local Hittites to secure a burial place. The custom of the day required that a person be buried in the ancestral homeland (cf. 49:29; 50:25). But by burying Sarah in Canaan, Abraham was boldly declaring this new land to be his home just as God had promised. Abraham was not negotiating for a place to dig a hole in the ground; caves were used as resting places for the remains of family members.

The Hittites' offer to allow Abraham to bury his dead in any of their tombs (v. 6) seems gracious, but it could be a cover for something else. One interpretative option is to say that they wanted to haggle the purchase price. But it is also true that people of the ancient Near East were often reluctant to sell their land to outsiders (cf. 1 Kgs. 21:3). Ephron's offer of the land as a free gift may have been to prevent Abraham from actually obtaining permanent ownership. He isn't a native, so he shouldn't own land—this was the mindset of the day.

But the patriarch proved persistent and seemingly didn't blink when Ephron named his price. It's impossible for us to know for sure the exact value of Abraham's 400 shekels of silver, but the price seems exorbitant. By means of comparison, the standard annual wage of a laborer at this time was a mere ten shekels. David purchased the threshing floor of Araunah and oxen to sacrifice there for a total of fifty silver shekels (2 Sam. 24:24); Jeremiah purchased a field from his cousin for 17 shekels (Jer. 32:9). If he had wanted to save the money, Abraham would have had the option to lease the land, but he instead wanted to pay the full price so as to secure the land for himself and his descendants in perpetuity. The sale was thereby indubitable.

This passage reads much like a typical real estate transaction record from antiquity. The Hebrew phrase translated "according to the weights current among the merchants" is almost identical to that used in other ancient contracts, as is the explicit stipulation that the trees be included in the sale. Such tells us that this chapter has importance beyond being an account of the burial of the great Hebrew matriarch.

It is significant for us to realize that this cave will be the first and only plot of land owned by Abraham. That's it—a cemetery! And that sole detail is the perfect capstone to Abraham's journey of faith. His call to leave Haran had begun with a promise of land, one reiterated when Lot separated, and reiterated yet again after defeating Chedor-laomer in battle. God had elaborately sworn that he would give this land to Abraham and his descendants, albeit after 400 years. And the patriarch had responded to that promise in faith.

So much faith, in fact, that he was willing to pay a ridiculous price for a field so that he could bury his wife in this promised land and thereby renounce his citizenship in the one he had left behind. In buying this cave, the patriarch was saying to God, "Lord, I believe you will indeed give this plot of ground, and much more, to my posterity." Abraham expressed his faith with a burial; God would fulfill his promise with a resurrection (Heb. 11:39-40).

Read Genesis 24. At this point, Abraham is 140 years old; he will live for another 35 years, but he did not know that. The text makes clear in no uncertain terms that he is a blessed man. So how does a blessed man behave when there is one final concern before death?

Scripture answers that question for us: he trusts unequivocally in the providence of God. Abraham's wealth is a prominent feature in this chapter, and he gave the command to use his wealth in whatever way necessary to secure for Isaac a good wife. The patriarch had no pretension of hanging on to his wealth indefinitely, or of taking it with him in death. Nor did he intend to spend it on himself. Rather, Abraham became the father of all those determined to spend their wealth to further the purposes of God.

For a special mission, the patriarch called to his side "his servant, the oldest of his household" (v. 2), and this has been commonly assumed to be Eliezer, the servant mentioned in 15:2. However, we cannot be sure since the servant remains anonymous throughout the narrative.

Abraham did not want Isaac to marry a Canaanite woman because of their immoral values. Esau would later displease Isaac by doing this (26:35). Not only was this Abraham's desire, but he also believed it was God's will. So the patriarch was convinced an angel would go with his servant and direct events to a favorable end.

Thus the servant set out on his mission, and nothing is said about the actual journey, one that would have taken at least a month. Arriving at the well in the city of Nahor, the servant began to beseech the God of Abraham. His prayer expresses remarkable faith in God. He essentially asks God to make his will known through a verifiable sign, and that is exactly what happens! In fact, so remarkable is God's faithfulness and providence that he began revealing his will "before [the servant] had finished speaking" (v. 15).

The sign the servant sought wasn't really a conspicuous miracle, but a noted oddity—something in the realm of possibility, but unlikely at the same time. One thirsty camel having gone several days without water can drink as much as 25 gallons of water, meaning Rebekah would have drawn her pitcher 80–100 times to satisfy all ten. And since it would have taken each camel at least ten minutes to drink its allotted amount, this chore would have taken almost two hours!

The genealogy of 22:20-24 already informed us that Abraham's brother Nahor had fathered a son named Bethuel, who in turn had fathered a daughter named Rebekah. When the servant realized God had providentially led him to Abraham's family as the source of Isaac's wife, he was overjoyed and offered up praise. It is notable that he gave thanks for Yahweh's "steadfast love" (v. 27), the term used throughout the Old Testament for God's covenant love for his people. In other words, the servant praised Yahweh for being faithful to his covenant with Abraham.

From here, the narrative moves quickly before slowing down again. Rebekah "ran" to tell her family what had happened, and her brother Laban "ran" to greet the man at the spring. The sight of such expensive jewelry on his sister told Laban that a very wealthy suitor was vying for her hand in marriage. In the ancient Near East, it was not uncommon for the brother to negotiate the marriage of his sister (rather than the parents), and Laban certainly assumed that role in this narrative, while Rebekah's parents seem to be secondary participants at best (cf. vv. 50, 55).

The servant and Rebekah departed the next morning. The servant knew that the God of his master Abraham had blessed his journey thus far, so he did not want to tarry any longer in returning to the patriarch lest he lose that blessing. Rebekah is also to be commended for her willingness to travel such a long distance to marry Isaac. In the ancient Near East, for a woman to leave her family and travel so far to marry was to incur considerable risk. What if her husband was abusive or divorced her once she proved barren? The latter, as it turns out, would be Rebekah's lot for twenty years.

At the end of the narrative, we learn that Isaac was dwelling in the Negeb at this point, and it was his habit in the evenings "to meditate in the field" (v. 63). The Hebrew word translated "meditate" is difficult to translate since the word occurs only here, but it likely means "to complain, lament." Isaac was going out into the fields in the evenings to lament before God the death of his mother Sarah. The arrival of Rebekah, then, is portrayed as a significant provision of divine comfort. Her veiling herself as she met Isaac was her way of identifying herself as his bride-to-be.

APPLICATION

What About Cremation? Scripture does not give definitive guidance as to how we are to dispose of the dead. Some in the Bible were cremated (e.g. Achan, Josh. 7:25), but most of those individuals were under God's curse. Albert Mohler writes, "The early church rejected the pagan practice of cremation because of a belief that the body is to be respected. The early Christians observed the Roman pattern of cremation and agreed that it represented an intentional destruction of the human body — a belief that conflicted with the believers' understanding that death was to be understood as sleep, and that the dead are awaiting the resurrection to come." Our word "cemetery" comes from the Greek *koimeterion* and the Latin *coemeteria*, both literally meaning "sleeping place." I do not question the salvation of those who have been cremated, but this point is nonetheless worthy of further consideration. By burying his beloved Sarah in Canaan, rather than in their homeland, Abraham boldly asserted his faith in the promises of God. So we also, by being interred in the earth, declare our faith in the promises of God, including his oath that death is not the end (John 11:25), that there will one day be a resurrection (John 5:28–29), and that we will be with the Lord forever (1 Thess. 4:17).

Unequally Yoked. Abraham's refusal to allow Isaac to marry a Canaanite woman bears a principle worth emulating. The Law of Moses warned Israel of the danger in intermarrying with her neighbors (Deut. 7:3–4), and when Solomon disobeyed this command, it was widely considered the beginning of the end for the glorious kingdom of Israel (cf. 1 Kgs. 11:4; Neh. 13:26). In the New Testament, Paul forbids a widow from marrying outside of the Lord (1 Cor. 7:39), and in general warns of being "yoked with unbelievers" (2 Cor. 6:14). I am in no way saying it is a sin to marry a non-Christian. But just because something is not a sin does not also mean it is wise (1 Cor. 6:12). We can look around a church auditorium and single out a handful of those who were brought to obedient faith in Christ through the influence of a godly spouse. But we must also acknowledge the dozens more who were led away from their faith by an ungodly spouse. We tend to forget about the ones who are no longer among us. As a consequence of the Fall, marriage is complicated as it is. Why unnecessarily make it more so?

Trust God in the Process. There is a great deal parents can learn from Abraham's example in Gen. 24. I'm not sure I want to return to the days when parents arranged marriages for their children, but neither does our culture, where shows like *The Bachelor* and *The Bachelorette* are a hit with television audiences, have much wisdom to offer in this regard. Parents would perform a great service to their children (and to the church) by lifting them up in prayer. Why not, from their birth, pray for the future mates of your children? Pray for God's guidance as you raise someone's future spouse, and that God would likewise guide the parents of your future son- or daughter-in-law. Pray that your daughter is as passionate about being Mrs. Right as she is about finding Mr. Right. Above all, affirm to your heavenly Father his sovereignty over all things—for your sake, not his (cf. Prov. 3:5-6).

CONCLUSION

As I reflect on these two chapters, it occurs to me that how we go about our daily responsibilities matters a great deal in the grand scheme of things. Ordinary, everyday traditions such as burial practices and showing hospitality matter. Abraham demonstrated his trust in God by how he buried Sarah and how he sought a wife for Isaac. Rebekah demonstrated her obedience by giving water to a traveler and his camels, to say nothing of her willingness to travel to a land far away and marry a man she had never met. The tone we take with friends, the courtesy we show our waiter, the choices we make as to how to spend our time or money—these can prove vitally important in our efforts to enlarge the boundaries of God's kingdom. "Trust and obey for there is no other way to be happy in Jesus."

QUESTIONS FOR REFLECTION

1. In Abraham's day, where was a person customarily buried?

2. Why were the Hittites reluctant to sell land to Abraham? Why did Abraham so willingly pay such an exorbitant price for the land?

3. By burying Sarah in Canaan, what statement was Abraham making concerning his faith?

4. Why was Abraham so intent on finding a wife for Isaac outside of Canaan?

5. Why was Abraham confident that his servant would be successful?

6. What was the servant's response when the mission indeed proved successful?

QUESTIONS FOR DISCUSSION

1. Should a Christian prefer bodily burial to cremation? Why/why not?

2. In what ways do you see God's providence at work in the story of Gen. 24?

3. What difficulties are caused in marriage when couples do not share the same spiritual values?

4. What can parents do to demonstrate their faith in God when it comes to securing a good spouse for their child?

5. In what specific ways can you grow in showing faith in God and his promises in the everyday events and habits of life?

13

THE DEATH OF ABRAHAM

GENESIS 25

Objective: To memorialize Abraham's life
and review the lessons he teaches us

INTRODUCTION

How is it that the father of the fearful can become the father of the faithful? We have a habit of approaching the lives of God's saints with awe and wonder, and we place them on a pedestal, foolishly believing "I could never be like them." We have seen Abraham's frailty and weakness time and again throughout his life. But God was faithful to Abraham through many dangers, toils, and snares, and eventually Abraham learned to trust in the person and promises of God.

Abraham's life—both his spiritual successes and his failures—should inspire us in our own lives of faith. As we reflect on Abraham's life in his final moments, we are aware that God has indeed made his name great. Abraham is wealthy. Abraham is happy. Abraham now has many, many sons—and not just biologically. For everyone who trusts in God, they too become a child of Abraham and a fellow heir to his promises (Rom. 4:16).

EXAMINATION

Read Genesis 25:1-11. Sometime after the death of Sarah, Abraham married a woman named Keturah, and by her the patriarch fathered six sons. Of these sons and their descendants, most are unknown to history, and attempts by a few scholars to identity them often prove problematic. Many of these clans settled in northern Arabia on the fringes of the Negeb, but that's as much as we know for certain. But of the sixteen sons and grandsons that came from Keturah, here is how a few of them fit into latter developments in the Old Testament.

Nothing is known about Jokshan, but it's a different story concerning his son. Sheba became a nation in southwest Arabia, and its queen visited Jerusalem during the reign of Solomon (1 Kgs. 10:1-13). Sheba's brother, Dedan, also settled in Arabia. Dedan was also a place in northwest Arabia that became an important commercial center. It is assumed that the descendants of Dedan's three sons populated the place Dedan, but beyond that, very, very little is known about Asshurim, Letushim, and Leummim.

However, of Abraham's fourth son by Keturah, we know a good bit. The tribe of Midian is somewhat of an enigma in Scripture. They are portrayed as neutral traders later in the Joseph narrative (37:28), and Moses married into the family of Jethro, the priest of Midian (Exod. 3:1). But in Numbers, the Midianites and Moabites conspired against Israel (22:4-7; 25:1-9; 31:1-54), and in the Judges period, they are the antagonists in the story of Gideon (Judg. 6-8). Midian's first son, Ephah, may have gained notoriety as a camel breeder (cf. Isa. 60:6), and Assyrian records from the time of Tiglath-pileser III and Sargon II mention Ephah as a tribe in northwest Arabia. Of Midian's other five sons, virtually nothing else is certain.

The sixth son of Abraham and Keturah was Shuah. One of Job's three friends is Bildad the Shuhite (Job 2:11). The land of Shuah may be the same as Suhu, an Assyrian province, and a summer pasture for Arabian tribes during the reign of the Assyrian king Sargon II (722–705 B.C.).

Before he died, Abraham bequeathed all he had to Isaac. He had already sent Ishmael away at Sarah's behest. Now he sent his other six sons away "to the east country," i.e. the desert region just east of the land of Israel. We can assume that he sent them away as regretfully as he had Ishmael; Abraham seems to have been a man with a lot of love for his family. He gave gifts to Keturah's six sons, which was extraordinarily generous since he technically owed them nothing. But the larger point is that he sent them away so that Isaac could receive everything and also dwell alone in the Promised Land. Even to his death, Abraham was committed to living out his faith in the promises of God.

As was made clear in Gen. 5, death is a fate from which none of us can escape, not even Abraham. But if we have to die, what better condition can we ask for than the one Abraham experienced? The narrator says that the patriarch passed "at a ripe old age, old and contented, and he was gathered to his people" (v. 8 HCSB). He had experienced many blessings and had become, by the power of God, a father of many nations (17:5). But Abraham died not having received all of God's blessings or realizing all of his promises. Even now, those promises await a fulfillment at the end of time when you and I will be made perfect with Abraham (Heb. 11:39-40).

But the story doesn't end with Abraham's death. Yet another of Genesis' "Hallmark moments" is narrated here. Though separated when they were just boys, Ishmael and Isaac had apparently stayed in contact. They now came together in peace to bury their beloved father beside the body of Sarah in the family cemetery, the cave of

Machpelah. After the funeral, the narrator is careful to say that God began to bless Isaac as he had his father. In the previous chapter, we had been told that Isaac had dwelt for some time at Beer-lahai-roi before returning to the Negeb (24:62). Now he returned to Beer-lahai-roi, the place where God had previously heard and answered Hagar's prayer (16:14). As a man of prayer, Isaac wanted to be in a place where he could commune with God and have his petitions heard.

Read Genesis 25:12-18. As the narrator has done before, he does so here: he dispenses with the non-elect lineage (Cain, Japheth, Ham) before continuing the story. Like his nephew Jacob, Ishmael was blessed with twelve sons who became "princes" of their respective tribes, or better translated "chiefs." God had promised Hagar that her son would become "a great nation" (21:18), and this genealogy is proof that God's promise was fulfilled.

As with the sons of Keturah, we do not know a whole lot about Ishmael's sons. The tribes settled in the Sinai and Arabian peninsulas (v. 18); some make appearances in the preaching of Isaiah, Jeremiah, and Ezekiel. Many of these names are also mentioned in the Assyrian records of Tiglath-pileser III and Ashurbanipal, and the Babylonian records of Nebuchadnezzar and Nabonidus. Kedar became the most powerful of the Ishmaelite tribes. Nebuchadnezzar led a campaign against Arabian tribes in 599 B.C., and Kedar seems to have been among his conquests (Jer. 49:28-33). In Ezek. 27:21, Kedar is said to be a trading partner with Tyre.

Before his birth, it had been prophesied that Ishmael would "dwell over against all his kinsmen" (16:12). That promise is also fulfilled (v. 18).

The rest of Gen. 25 will be covered in the next volume of this study,* Genesis 26-50 from Start2Finish. *

CONCLUSION

Take a moment to step back from Abraham's life and appreciate how far he has come. In the beginning, he showed great promise by following God to Canaan. But in so many other ways, he struggled to trust in the promises of God. Until Gen. 22, the patriarch's life had been characterized by as many failures as successes.

And now that I mention it, these failures make me wonder about the legitimacy of Paul's statement concerning Abraham in Rom. 4:20-21. "No unbelief made him waver concerning the promise of God, but he grew strong in his faith as he gave glory to God, fully convinced that God was able to do what he had promised." I'm not in the habit of disagreeing with inspired writers, but Paul seems to be fuzzy on the facts. Have we not seen clear examples of Abraham's numerous failings in faith? Have we not seen indisputable evidence that he did waver, that he did doubt that God had power to do what he promised? How do we reconcile Abraham's life with Paul's words?

Perhaps an old woodsmen's proverb can resolve this tension. As he was authoring his famous biography on the life of Abraham Lincoln, Carl Sandburg searched in vain for an appropriate title for the chapter detailing with the immediate aftermath of Lincoln's assassination. What one phrase could adequately express the aftermath of that dark moment in our nation's history? Sandburg was at a loss until he discovered this old woodsmen's proverb: "A tree is best measured when it's down."

God looks at our lives with a wide-angle lens, not a telephoto zoom. The final verdict will not be rendered on our life until the end of our life. Our tree will not be measured until it's lying down. God did not strike Abraham dead when he first lied about his relationship with Sarah, nor did he send fire from heaven when Ishmael was conceived. Rather, God sought to create in Abraham, to borrow a phrase from

Friedrich Nietzsche, "a long obedience in the same direction." The life of faith is a marathon, not a sprint.

Have you stumbled? Pause and regain your balance.

Have you fallen? Get up. The race is not over.

This is why Paul could write concerning Abraham, "He did not waver through unbelief regarding the promise of God," and that the patriarch was "fully convinced that God was able to do what he had promised." Paul could write those words because this was the divine verdict when Abraham's tree was measured lying down. Though it took him more than a hundred years to get there, Abraham finally learned that God provides, that he will do what he has promised. The patriarch learned that it is God who supplies all of our needs (Phil. 4:19).

QUESTIONS FOR REFLECTION

1. Who did Abraham marry after Sarah's death and how many sons did he have by her?

2. Who was Keturah's fourth son and why was he significant?

3. What inheritance did these sons receive, and why did Abraham send them away?

4. Describe briefly the fate of Ishmael and his descendants, especially in relation to Israel.

5. How can Rom. 4:20-21 be reconciled with all the details of Abraham's life?

QUESTIONS FOR DISCUSSION

1. "The life of faith is a marathon, not a sprint." Explain what this statement means to you.

2. Why is it important to realize that God does not make a final judgment on our lives until the end of our lives?

3. In what ways are Christians heirs to Abraham's promises of property, prosperity, and protection?

4. If we never succeed in trusting God's providence and promises, can we ever be happy in life? Explain your answer.

5. What is the most important lesson you have gained from studying Abraham's life? How are you living your Christian life differently as a result of that lesson?

PERSONAL NOTES

PERSONAL NOTES

PERSONAL NOTES

PERSONAL NOTES

PERSONAL NOTES

PERSONAL NOTES

PERSONAL NOTES

PERSONAL NOTES

PERSONAL NOTES

PERSONAL NOTES

PERSONAL NOTES

PERSONAL NOTES

PERSONAL NOTES

SUGGESTED RESOURCES

Longman, Tremper, III. *How to Read Genesis*. Downers Grove, IL: Inter-Varsity Press, 2005.

Waltke, Bruce. *Genesis*. Grand Rapids: Zondervan, 2001.

Walton, John H. *Genesis*. Grand Rapids: Zondervan, 2000.

Whitworth, Michael. *The Epic of God*. Bowie, TX: Start2Finish, 2012.

ABOUT THE AUTHOR

MICHAEL WHITWORTH is the owner of Start2Finish and ministers for the church of Christ in Keller, Texas. He is the author of several books, including the award-winning *The Epic of God* and *The Derision of Heaven*.

He considers M&Ms his brain food and is fond of large Mason jars. In his spare time, Michael loves reading and drinking coffee, watching sports, and spending time with his family and furry golden retriever.

To order additional Bible Studies from Start2Finish, visit start2finish.org/bible-studies, call (888) 978-3850, or ask for them at your favorite Christian bookstore.

Also available for Kindle, Nook, & iBooks.

Made in the USA
San Bernardino, CA
16 February 2016